Michael Perham has been Bishop of Gloucester since 2004, and before that was Dean of Derby. He was one of the architects of the Church of England's *Common Worship*, and has written widely on liturgy, theology and spirituality. He is Bishop Protector of the Society of St Francis and Chair of the Governing Body of both Ripon College Cuddesdon and SPCK.

D0620533

TO TELL AFRESH

Michael Perham

First published in Great Britain in 2010

Society for Promoting Christian Knowledge
36 Causton Street
London SW1P 4ST
www.spckpublishing.co.uk

British Library Cataloguing-in-Publication Data
A catalogue record for this book is available from the British Library

ISBN 978–0–281–06231–7

1 3 5 7 9 10 8 6 4 2

Typeset by Graphicraft Ltd, Hong Kong
Printed in Great Britain by Ashford Colour Press

Produced on paper from sustainable forests

*For the people of the Diocese of Gloucester
and for their clergy,
with whom it is my joy and privilege to serve
as bishop*

Contents

Preface

There is a legal document in the Church of England that bishops often find themselves reading aloud. It is the Preface to the Declaration of Assent that every minister has to make before ordination or admission to a new ministry. It traces the story of what down the centuries has shaped the belief of Anglicans, through Scripture, through creeds and through particular historical and liturgical documents dating from the Reformation. And then it says that this faith is to be proclaimed 'afresh in each generation' ('The Declaration of Assent', *Common Worship*). Whenever I read that Preface, those words stand out for me. The faith of the Church, at one level unchanging, has to be proclaimed afresh in each generation. A bishop, because of his ministry as a guardian of the faith, has a particular responsibility and privilege, speaking out of a generous orthodoxy, to do that, to find the words to make what Mark's Gospel calls 'the sacred and imperishable proclamation of eternal salvation' reasonable, accessible and attractive to all who are prepared to engage with it (Mark 16, shorter ending).

It is too easy for this teaching ministry to be squeezed out by all the other tasks the Church lays upon its bishops, but I have tried to give priority to talking with people about the faith that shapes my own life. I have tried to be faithful to my understanding of what I believe the Church has always taught, but I have tried also to share something of my own much more personal encounter with God and my own engagement with Christian doctrine. In particular I have, several years running, invited people in different deaneries of the Diocese of Gloucester to meet with me during Lent to explore this faith that needs to be proclaimed afresh in each generation.

When we have met, we have celebrated the Eucharist together, rooting our exploration in worship and prayer, then had a gap so that others who might want to explore without a personal commitment to prayer and worship might join us, then had a fairly substantial presentation by me and, finally, had a time of question and discussion. Several hundred people have taken part in these evenings over a period of three years. The origin of this book lies in those presentations. Five of the eight chapters that follow were talks given in that series. Three more have been added to create a more complete picture of the faith that excites and energizes me.

I am grateful to all those who encouraged me to make this material available to a wider audience. I am thankful also for all those who engage with me theologically, in a variety of settings, and thus contribute to my understanding of the Christian faith. I carry also a deep gratitude to those who worship with me in the cathedral and churches of the Diocese of Gloucester, for it is in prayer and worship that I am enabled to enter more deeply into the mystery of God.

Over the years, and since long before I became Chair of its Governing Body, I have received huge encouragement in my writing from SPCK, the publishing arm of which has been my publisher for 30 years. To its staff, and especially to Joanna Moriarty, its Publishing Director, I owe a particular debt of gratitude.

My hope is that, for some at least, this book will speak afresh of the Christian faith and so be part of its proclamation to this generation.

+Michael Gloucester:

1

I believe in an amazing God

There is something very pleasing about systematic theology, everything set out in a satisfying developing order, one thing related to another, no area of belief left uncovered and unexplored. But this book is not a systematic presentation of the Christian gospel, because it is bound to be very selective and huge areas of Christian faith won't even get a mention. That does not mean that they are unimportant, but you cannot say everything and I am going for the issues that make the concept of God most real for me, making relationship with God a possibility.

There is always a bit of a tension between 'I believe' and 'we believe'. Both are important. The 'we believe' is the faith of the Church, the faith handed down, something we have to take on trust, while exploring it for ourselves and testing it out in our own Christian experience. The Nicene Creed is the great 'we believe' profession of faith, for its origins lie in the collective wisdom of the Church, struggling with doctrine and then coming to something of a consensus. This is what the Church believes. A bishop's task is to uphold that faith and to do it in such a way that it is commended to others, made intelligible afresh in each generation.

'I believe' is just a little bit different from that. First of all, it is personal testimony that this faith that I have received, which I share with the whole Christian community, is nevertheless personal. I have made it my own. The great 'I believe' profession of faith is that other creed, the Apostles' Creed, which has its origins in baptism, where the individual stands alone before the water and makes their personal profession. But 'I believe' also gives a clue to what it is, in the vast Christian tradition, that lights up a particular individual, that excites them, that makes God real for them. And what I want to do in these chapters is to share some of the truths and insights of the Christian tradition that most excite me. But it will all be highly selective.

There will be talk about God – theology – in every chapter, even when the title comes from a different angle. But I want to begin, as I will want to end, with some explicit exploration of the one who is for me an amazing God.

I want to make and develop four affirmations about God, to try to bring some clarity to the issue of God and gender, and to give notice of two other affirmations that will be explored in later chapters.

First, I believe in a holy God. That's really an understatement. I believe in a God who is all holiness, holiness beyond our imagining. It seems to be the right place to start, for whatever else we go on to say about God, making stabs at explaining God, we need with a proper humility to recognize that God is beyond our comprehension. God is unutterable beauty. God is dazzling holiness. God is wholly other. God is clothed in mystery. There are some other things to say later that might seem to modify that, but this is what I want to affirm for now. When we look at the Christ-likeness of God we find ourselves engaging with a God who reveals himself, a God with whom we may be intimate. But none of that ought ever to obscure the important truth that God is awesome, wondrous mystery and that silence in God's presence is usually better than words. If God were anything less than awesome, wondrous mystery, he would not be God. Most of the time we allow our God to be too small. Too often our picture of God does not do God justice. It is Christian worship that can keep reminding us just how great our God is and to that we will return.

I need at this point to go off on a tangent, just to clear something up. It is the 'God and gender' issue, because even to write these paragraphs I have been struggling to talk about God without committing myself on divine gender. I've almost managed it, but one 'himself' has slipped in. I am entirely orthodox on the gender of God, but a lot of good Christian people are not as orthodox as they think they are. They say things like, 'I don't know what all this fuss about inclusive language is all about; it's just political correctness; everyone knows God is male.'

God is not male. Nor is God female. God is beyond gender. Genesis has an important theological insight when it tells us that God created the human race in his image: in Genesis 1.27 we read, 'male and female he created them'. All that we understand as masculine and all that we understand as feminine is derived from God and is part of the image of God implanted in us, God who is beyond gender, for God is God.

But we have a language problem when we come to pronouns. If God is beyond gender, can I speak of him as 'he' or 'she' or 'it'? Because God is personal, a being with whom I can be in relationship, it is important that I do not speak of God as 'it', which makes God less than personal and less than God. 'He' or 'she' is infinitely better. The Christian tradition, arising out of the Jewish faith, opts for 'he', not least because Jesus calls God 'Father'. The Scriptures reveal to us a norm of speaking of God as 'he', but the attributes of God include those that we more normally associate with the feminine. God is portrayed as a consoling, nursing, mothering God, just as much as God is portrayed as a battling, ruling, correcting God. So in Isaiah we read:

> Rejoice with Jerusalem, and be glad for her,
> all you who love her;
> rejoice with her in joy, all you who mourn over her –
> that you may nurse and be satisfied from her consoling breast;
> that you may drink deeply with delight from her glorious bosom.
>
> For thus says the LORD:
> I will extend prosperity to her like a river,
> and the wealth of the nations like an overflowing stream;
> and you shall nurse and be carried on her arm,
> and dandled on her knees.
> As a mother comforts her child, so I will comfort you.
> (Isaiah 66.10–13)

So the Church is content to call God 'he' and regard that as the norm, but fairly relaxed about the fact that sometimes people will want to explore what it means to call God 'she', even in prayer, especially when they have experienced a patriarchal way of talking of God as oppressive.

Jesus Christ, of course, was a man, a male. That may not be entirely unimportant in understanding the nature of God, but the maleness of Jesus is not nearly as important as the humanity of Jesus. When we say in the Creed that Jesus 'was made man', what we are saying is that God became a human being. That he became a male human being is secondary.

So, coming back to my main theme, I will proceed to talk of God as 'God', but occasionally as 'he', with a shared understanding that God is beyond gender.

Second, I believe in a Creator God. I need to confess that I have an artistic mind, not a scientific one. I can probably accept more easily than some the belief that there is no fundamental conflict between the Christian understanding of creation and the insights of the scientists. For me the existence of an intelligence behind creation is the most natural thing in all the world to believe. And every fresh and fascinating discovery by scientists, whether it be about our solar system or our planet or about the human mind and body, reinforces for me that there is pattern, order and intention in the creation. I believe in a Creator God and I believe that the opening words of the Bible are spot on – 'In the beginning God'.

There is an attitude to Scripture that we often label 'fundamentalist', though to be fair that can be a crude lumping together of a variety of views that have in common that they take the Bible very literally. 'This is just the way it was,' the fundamentalist says, 'historically, scientifically, factually.' Of course, fundamentalism is not just about attitudes to the early chapters of Genesis, but it is around this issue of how the world came into being that most of the fuss has centred, ever since Darwin and the theory of evolution, and here the fundamentalist becomes the 'creationist'. Probably only a very small minority of Christians in our culture want to insist that, as a matter of historical and scientific fact, the world was made in six days or that the human race was placed on the earth much like it is now, rather than emerging from a more primitive form of life. But so ineffectively have Christians proclaimed their faith that most of the world outside assumes that this is what we believe.

If I were setting out to tell a bit of history, I would not give you two versions and claim them both to be true, because I would know that involved contradiction. Nor, if I wanted to convince you of a scientific fact, would I give you two alternative theories and invite you to make a choice. But the editor of Genesis gives you two versions. This is surely because he is not trying to describe a bit of history or to give you a scientific explanation. He is not a historian and he is not a scientist. He has no great interest or competence in either of those disciplines. He has a different sort of mind altogether.

He is more of an artist. As an artist he might well paint two pictures, looking at the same scene in two quite different ways. He might adopt different styles that drew out different things. He could certainly hang his two pictures side by side and let you see their differences, without you having to say which one was true.

Yes, the editor of Genesis was more like an artist than a scientist or a historian. He was painting pictures of creation and asking you to let them speak to you something of the truth. In reality, though this is true, he is more than an artist, for the truths he wants you to latch on to are essentially about God. He is, in the end, a theologian. What he is trying to do is to convey deep truths about God, about the world and about the human race. Truths like these.

First, 'In the beginning God.' It matters not how the world was made, how long it took, what scientific processes were part of it. Scientific accounts of these will change as new knowledge comes to light and inadequate theories are discarded. But it does matter that, behind it all, there is the hand of God. Before anything came to be, there was God. God is the beginning. God is the origin. God is the source. The universe was created at his word. That is the theological truth that shines through these stories. It does not explain everything, but it gives Christians their starting point in dialogue with others.

Second, the creation was not chance or accident. It was meant to be. It was part of a divine plan, the beginning of God's scheme of things. It was – it is – God's grand design, and there is shape, pattern, order to the universe. Nothing is entirely random. Chaos has been tamed. That too shines through these stories and, again, it is a theological truth of deep significance.

Third, the human race is the summit of God's creation. The two stories tell it differently, but it is the same truth. Whether, as in Genesis 1, humankind comes at the end of the creation process, or as in Genesis 2 at the beginning, the truth is that the human race is not just another species of an animal kingdom, but a race that is special, that is in a unique relationship with the Creator, that is central to his purpose for the world: a race that is made in the image of God. When thinking about God as Creator it does not matter whether either Genesis story has got it scientifically right or whether we are indeed descended from the fish or the apes. It does matter that God has looked upon the human race and called it into a unique relationship with him. It does matter that God has made us a little like himself.

Fourth, it is not only men, but women, who are created in the image of God. 'God created man' – that is, humankind – 'in his own image . . . male and female created he them' (AV). That's not some modern feminist bit of theology. As I mentioned earlier, it's straight out of Genesis. A woman is in the image of God as much as a man. Christian history has rarely done justice to that truth, but there it is, stated right at the beginning.

Fifth, work is good and rest is good. For six symbolic days God worked. On the seventh day God rested. And he ordained that as a pattern for the human race. Work and rest, labour and leisure, are both part of the human destiny. We are to 'do', but we are also to have time simply to 'be'. One of the Ten Commandments, to keep holy the sabbath, arises out of the original picture in Genesis of a God who himself worked and rested, and it is, of course, a truth relevant for today. In a world of high unemployment, we have to say that the right to work is part of our human vocation, though what form this work may take in our society may be very different from what we have known. And in a world of hyperactivity, we have to say that pleasure and leisure are part of God's will for us also.

Sixth, the human race is placed by God in a unique relationship to the creation, yet not as owner or exploiter but as a steward. We are to enjoy the creation, but we are to treat it with reverence, to recognize it as God's and to cooperate with him in the process of renewing it. Any sort of theology of conservation finds its roots here in the Genesis accounts of creation.

What does all this add up to? A Creator God, who is working still.

If Genesis begins with God, John's Gospel begins with 'the Word': 'In the beginning was the Word, and the Word was with God, and the Word was God.' We are into a different world and the difference is Jesus Christ. If we are to enter into the mystery of God's being, to penetrate his nature, so that we can speak of him intelligently and love him confidently, then we need a clue to his character: and that clue – more than a clue, a revelation – is Jesus Christ, whom the apostle Paul tells us in Colossians is the very image of God.

> He is the image of the invisible God, the firstborn of all creation; for in him all things in heaven and on earth were created, things visible and invisible, whether thrones or dominions or rulers or powers – all things have been created through him and for him . . . For in him all the fullness of God was pleased to dwell.   (Colossians 1.15–16, 19)

In chapter 14 of his Gospel the evangelist John assures us, in words on the lips of Jesus himself, that to have seen Jesus is to have seen the Father. To know Jesus is to know God.

The insistence of Christian orthodoxy that Jesus is not just a holy man, a good teacher, a miracle worker and a moral exemplar, but the Son of God in a unique way, is important not just because we want to know Jesus for who he was and is but because we want to know God for who he is. Unless Jesus is divine, all we can learn from him is something about his own character. But if he is himself part of the Godhead, inextricably linked with the Father, then he is the one who shows us God.

So, if we search the Gospels, what do we learn from the life of Jesus about the character of God? It is difficult to know where to start, let alone where to end. But let me choose just three adjectives and unpack each in turn. The Christ-like God is the humble God, the suffering God, the resurrecting God.

To speak of the humble God is to come first to the Incarnation. There are other moments when Jesus reveals the humility of God, as when he gets down on his knees and washes the disciples' feet, but the key moment is in his birth. Paul puts it magnificently, of course, in his great hymn in the letter to the Philippians:

> . . . though he was in the form of God,
> [he] did not regard equality with God
> as something to be exploited,
> but emptied himself,
> taking the form of a slave,
> being born in human likeness.
> And being found in human form,
> he humbled himself . . .
>   (Philippians 2.6–8)

Paul goes on to speak of humbling himself in becoming obedient to the death of the cross. But the fundamental act of humility is in laying divinity aside, emptying himself, to become one of us. It is why the manger scene at Christmas is so powerful. Here is the Lord of heaven and earth, the Creator God, cloaked in mystery, suddenly become a crying baby in a cattle shed. The thought that the one whom we call 'almighty' and 'omnipotent' is a humble servant-God goes on being a surprise. We are always wanting to put God on a pedestal, safely beyond our reach. But a Christ-like God jumps down from the pedestal and will not climb on to it again. And so we begin to meet the God with whom we can be intimate, the God more like a friend or a lover than a lord and a master. This is a God with whom you might without too much difficulty share your vulnerability and even discover his. This is the humble God who challenges so much of the way we ordinarily speak of him. A Christ-like God is a humble God.

Paul in Philippians moves us very quickly from the Incarnation to the death of Jesus 30 years later. 'Being found in human form, he humbled himself' – and he adds immediately – 'and became obedient to the point of death – even death on a cross.' That brings us to the thought of the suffering God. This is difficult and I want to explore it quite carefully. The suffering of Jesus we all know about. The Passion narratives in the Gospels reveal a Jesus who entered fully into the human experiences of rejection, isolation, betrayal and pain. On the cross there was a loss of dignity and in some reading of the Scriptures a loss of the sense of God himself. The crucifix, as we normally see it, shows us a suffering Jesus, and a Jesus suffering for a purpose: that by his obedience and his sacrifice he might open up a path for suffering humanity to come back to God. We could spend a long time on the suffering of Jesus and still not exhaust the theological theories about the atonement.

But the suffering of God? Can we talk of that? Christian orthodoxy through the centuries has played it down. It has preferred to put an emphasis on God's impassibility – a word that means that God is incapable of suffering or feeling pain. The man Jesus, the one who had emptied himself of divinity, could and did suffer, but almighty God could not and does not. That was the theological emphasis through much of Christian history. But there has always been another strand of theology that has seen it rather differently, one that in a sense came into its own in the twentieth century as people struggled to make sense of phenomena such as Auschwitz, Hiroshima, Biafra, Bosnia, and the tsunami of 2004, as well as of more personal human suffering: the child dying of cancer, the victims of terrible abuse. Always there are the questions, 'Where is God in that? Why does he stand idly by?'

The classic answer – there is nothing new here – is, of course, in relation to human free will. God has made us free agents, able to respond to him but also able to go our own fallen way. Sometimes we might wish God had made us otherwise, but in the end to be human, to be in God's image, is to have that free will to choose the good or to choose the evil. To be otherwise would make us pawns or puppets. And whenever we look at the tragedies of our world, we nearly always see human wickedness and folly, not divine activity. Even something like a famine or a tsunami that might be called an act of God turns out, more often than not, to be caused by human greed or the abuse of the creation; though there are still areas, when all is said and done, where we cannot identify human sin as the cause and then we wonder what kind of God we believe in.

Unless we believe in an interventionist God, who lays aside the very laws of nature that he has put in place or sweeps away the free will he has given to his children, we have a God who simply looks on. Can we cope with the idea of an inscrutable God who simply watches unmoved, feeling no passion and no pain? Increasingly the twentieth century could not believe that of God. Increasingly it talked of a passionate God, a vulnerable God, a suffering God, a God who weeps, a God of weakness.

And if the Incarnation tells us something not just about the humility of Jesus but about the humility of God, then the atonement tells us something not just about the suffering of Jesus but about the suffering of God. What Jesus showed on the cross was a God who suffers with us and for us.

This sort of theology, to which I am much drawn, despite some difficult questions it throws up about whether God can be both omnipotent and vulnerable, is expressed in some of the texts we use in worship. There is, for instance, the hymn by Timothy Rees:

And when human hearts are breaking
Under sorrow's iron rod,
Then they find the selfsame aching
Deep within the heart of God.
'God is love: let heaven adore him',
New English Hymnal

W. H. Vanstone's poem 'Love's endeavour, love's expense', at the end of his profoundly moving book of the same title, also captures this sense of the suffering God.

> Love that gives gives ever more,
> Gives with zeal, with eager hands,
> Spares not, keeps not, all outpours,
> Ventures all, its all expends.
>
> Drained is love in making full,
> Bound in setting others free;
> Poor in making many rich;
> Weak in giving power to be.
>
> Therefore he who thee reveals
> Hangs, O Father, on that tree
> Helpless; and the nails and thorns
> Tell of what thy love must be.
>
> Thou art God; no monarch thou
> Throned in easy state to reign;
> Thou art God, whose arms of love
> Aching, spent, the world sustain.
>
> W. H. Vanstone,
> *Love's Endeavour, Love's Expense*

The Christ-like God is the suffering God. But a Christ-like God is also a resurrecting God. If the birth of Jesus speaks to us of a humble God, the atonement of a suffering God, then Easter and the empty tomb also have a message for us about the character of God. The resurrection of Jesus – the bursting from the tomb because death could not hold him – is a unique event in human history, but resurrection is what God does. The God of the Christians is a subversive God and never more so than on Easter Day.

'Life gives way to death.' Isn't that the natural order? Look at our sadness when a great tree comes down in a storm and has to be sawn up and carried away. Look at our sorrow when a human being or even a much loved animal dies. And don't just look at physical decay and death, real as that is; look also at the seemingly inevitable pattern that everything that is good somehow goes sour or stale or out of fashion or declines. Cynical that may be, but it is the way the world thinks and it has quite a lot of evidence to back it up. But along comes Christian faith, faith in the God of surprises, the resurrecting

God, insisting that the world has got it wrong. It isn't that life gives way to death, but that death is the entrance to life. And it cites the Easter event as the most powerful piece of evidence for this counter-cultural view. Jesus died, and the tomb ought, in the world's way of thinking, to have been the end of it all, with the stone undisturbed; but not only did he come back to life, it was a life of so much greater quality, intensity and reality than the life before. It was and is eternal. He is with us, Christian experience tells us, wonderfully alive, till the end of time.

From that event we work out the implications. Resurrection becomes not simply a one-off event, but the way God works. When we die, our bodies may lie in the dust, but our souls live with God. And when, at various points in our life, we go through an experience of darkness or despair that seems death-like, that very depth of darkness and despair is the seed-bed of hope and life and resurrection. That is the Christian counter-cultural faith. The God of surprises is a resurrecting God. He can't stop doing it; it is the way he is.

Christian faith not only recognizes that truth, but invites people to embrace it wholeheartedly and let it shape their lives. For that is exactly what baptism is about: embracing Christ's counter-cultural way of dying to the old to rise to the new; being buried with Christ in order to be raised with him. It is the lifestyle that we have embraced, though it may take a lifetime to be truly conformed to this Christ-like way.

Yes, death gives way to life, not life gives way to death. Christian faith preaches subversive good news from the counter-cultural resurrecting God. He is eternal and unfading love, who draws life out of death, just because that is the way he has chosen to be. He did so supremely when he raised Jesus Christ from the dead.

God is, I believe, the God of the great reversal. In the face of darkness, God brings light. In the face of defeat, God brings victory. In the face of tragedy, God brings triumph. In the face of death, God brings life. Bringing life out of death is simply the way God is. God is always doing it. He can do no other. Resurrection is happening all the time in lives around us, and maybe sometimes in our own lives, if only we would open our eyes to see.

It happens when, out of experiences that feel death-like – the deep despair of a relationship that has broken down, a period for an artist or a musician where inspiration will not come, the loss of faith – there comes either the sudden sense of new life or hope, or, more likely, a gradual dawning, the sense of light at the end of a dark tunnel. The light is the light of the Risen Christ. It is the work of the Christ-like resurrecting God.

Alongside a God who can be experienced as holy, Creator and Christ-like, there is the animating God, the God who energizes us and gives us life. This emerges very naturally from talk of the resurrecting God, but Christian theology specifically identifies the giving of life with the Holy Spirit. It is that Holy Spirit whom I want to explore now. Jesus, in his conversation with the woman at the well, recorded in John 4.24, speaks of God as Spirit, but how are we to understand God as Spirit?

Scripture begins with the Spirit who hovers over the waters when the Creator God brings into being all that is to be.

> In the beginning when God created the heavens and the earth, the earth was a formless void and darkness covered the face of the deep, while a wind from God [some other versions read 'the Spirit of God'] swept over the face of the waters. (Genesis 1.1–2)

Before there is a human race, before there is a world as we know it, there is the Spirit, brooding, hovering, sweeping over the face of the waters. The Spirit is not the Christian Spirit; the Spirit is not even only the Spirit of Jesus. The Spirit is the Spirit of God and the Spirit's operation is the world. If the Spirit must have a home, then that home is nothing less than the whole created order.

The world is the sphere of the Spirit's influence not just through some ethereal or marginal hovering, somewhere a little distance from the rough and tumble of the world's life. The Spirit is at work in the events of human history. We talk about the 'human spirit' sometimes, but more profoundly it is the Spirit of the animating God, who blows like a wind, so often a wind of change, and reveals to men and women a little more of divine reality. Every age sees it in some new way. In our own day, I do not doubt that it is the Holy Spirit, conspiring with the human spirit, that has brought a fresh understanding of human dignity and broken down barriers between people of different colours and ethnic origins, giving us a broader, more inclusive picture of the richness of the human race. Nor do I doubt that it is the Holy Spirit, conspiring with the human spirit, that has begun to free womankind to reach her potential – woman made in the image of God as much as man. The Spirit of God leads us into all truth with a divine impatience that so often forces the pace.

The Scriptures tell us next that God made the human race. He breathed into a man and a woman the breath of life. He gave them the Spirit. The image Genesis gives us of that first man and woman, into whom God breathed his Spirit, is a picture of the way humanity is. It is the very essence of being human to be held in life by the Spirit of God. The Scriptures tell a series of tales of men and women in whom the Spirit dwells to good effect. Supremely, of course, as the Old Covenant gives way to the New, there is the Spirit overshadowing Mary so that the Saviour might be born, and then the Spirit descending like a dove upon Jesus himself in the waters of the Jordan.

The picture is of the Spirit of God conspiring with the human spirit in love and creativity. The Spirit is in a person not because they are religious but because they are human. Without the Spirit of God they are dead; they cease to be. God is not selective in giving his Spirit. God may give different gifts to different people, but his Spirit is planted deep within everyone. For the Spirit is the life-giver, the animator.

We must not be surprised to find the Spirit of God in every person, not just in men and women of faith, let alone only in Christians. It is the Spirit of God who inspires every piece of creativity – in artist, musician, craftsman and writer – because it is a kind of reflection of the divine creativity at the heart of all things. It is the Spirit of God who inspires every instance of loving, between lovers, among friends, towards neighbours, because it is a kind of extension of the divine loving at the heart of all things.

The Spirit does, of course, have a special sphere of activity in the Church, and to that we will return, but it is the whole world that God desires to be a Spirit-filled community, as summed up in those wonderful words of Gerard Manley Hopkins in his poem, 'God's grandeur'.

> The world is charged with the grandeur of God . . .
> Because the Holy Ghost over the bent
> World broods with warm breast and with ah! bright wings.
> Gerard Manley Hopkins, in *The Faber Book of Religious Verse*

The animating God breathes life into his world by his Holy Spirit.

Talk of the Christ-like God and the animating God brings us to the mystery of the Holy Trinity: a puzzle and an obstacle for some, but for me a joy and delight. I need to say at the beginning that my faith is a Trinitarian one. Over and over again I am inspired by the thought of the Father loving the Son, the Son loving the Father and the Spirit as the love flowing between them. Trinitarian language will break out frequently in the chapters that follow, but I have chosen to keep until the final chapter rather more of my understanding of this mystery. If it waits until the end, it is because it is for me the deepest truth at the heart of all things.

That brings me finally to the last thing I wanted to say in this chapter about the character of the God in whom I believe. God is a personal God. God is not a person, any more than God is a male, but he is personal in the sense that we can have a relationship with him, not entirely unlike our relationship with those to whom we are closest in this life. With God, as with them, we can be open and honest and intimate and trusting. On God we can rely for love and encouragement and utter faithfulness. Of course, it remains a mind-blowing truth that God can know the unique you, call you by your name, hold you individually in his heart. I can't begin to understand that, but I can sense it, and experience it, especially when I am myself working at that relationship through prayer. Prayer is where I experience God and know myself to have a personal relationship with him – the Holy One, the Creator, the humble, suffering, resurrecting Christ-like God, the one who animates and gives life. It is to prayer that I turn in the next chapter.

2

I believe in a community of prayer

It is through prayer and worship that we enter into a relationship with God. We can explore what the Scriptures teach about him, engage with what others have said about him and reflect on all the intellectual arguments about his nature and his very existence. But if we are to enter into the mystery of his being, we do it by prayer: prayer that is, in the Christian understanding, always 'through Jesus Christ our Lord'. Prayer brings us to the Father. Jesus brings us to the Father. The two statements always need to stand together.

The classic invitation to prayer in the Christian tradition, which we use, for instance, in the Prayers of Intercession at the Eucharist, is Trinitarian.

> In the power of the Spirit and in union with Christ,
> let us pray to the Father.
> ('Forms of Intercession', *Common Worship*)

For me, who even after years of giving time to prayer am still no more than a novice at it, it is an encouragement to know that my praying is not so much my own as a climbing on board something that happens within the life of God himself. It is worth unpacking that before exploring how we might go about praying, and indeed what prayer is. What do we mean when we say that we pray 'in the power of the Spirit'?

The apostle Paul gives us a clue in the letter to the Romans. He writes:

> The Spirit helps us in our weakness; for we do not know how to pray as we ought, but that very Spirit intercedes with sighs too deep for words. And God, who searches the heart, knows what is the mind of the Spirit, because the Spirit intercedes for the saints according to the will of God. (Romans 8.26–27)

It is the Holy Spirit himself who prays within us, carrying us along, conforming our prayers to the will of God, giving shape and expression to them, sometimes in words, but more often without words. Or so Paul believes when he speaks of 'sighs too deep for words'. We can sometimes sense the Spirit at work in our praying: the sense that we are not in control, but are being drawn, directed and somehow shaped, even as we struggle to pray.

Paul is not entirely consistent about this Trinitarian activity. For as well as speaking of the Holy Spirit as intercessor, he also speaks a few verses later of Jesus himself as one who intercedes for us. Perhaps praying, like loving, is part of the relationship within the life of God. Certainly Christians have always pictured Jesus as intercessor. The letter to the Hebrews speaks of Jesus as a high priest, 'able for all time to save those who approach God through him, since he always lives to make intercession for them' (Hebrews 7.25).

This sense of Jesus as the one through whom we pray, which leads to so many prayers ending 'through Jesus Christ', has more than one level of meaning. First, it means that it is because of what Jesus reveals about God that we can approach the Father, confidently addressing him with a familiarity that calls him 'Abba'; we can do this because Jesus has revealed him as a generous and compassionate God. Second, there is the encouragement that Jesus prays alongside us, as our elder brother and our priest, so that we can indeed pray 'in union with Christ'. Third, crucially, we have access to the Father because Jesus has restored our relationship with the Father by his loving, self-giving self-sacrifice. We pray through him because in himself and in his body on the cross he has opened the way.

Prayer in the power of the Spirit in union with Christ is the classical norm. It is worth saying that it is not the only way to pray to God. Some people find it helpful to address at least some of their prayer directly to Jesus. A lot of Christian hymns and songs do this. So, occasionally, does the liturgy of the Church. 'Lamb of God, you take away the sin of the world,' we pray at the Eucharist, very directly addressing Jesus ('Breaking of the Bread', *Common Worship*). And there is a long tradition of invoking the Holy Spirit at key moments in the Church's life, as at the ordination of priests and bishops when we pray, 'Come, Holy Ghost, our souls inspire' ('A Form of Preparation', *Common Worship*). Prayer to the Son and prayer to the Spirit have their place. God does not want us to have only one way of engaging with him.

But what the classical approach to the Father, aided by the Son and the Spirit, amounts to – and it is a huge encouragement – is that we are never praying alone and we are never praying in our own power. The Spirit is praying within us. Jesus is, so to speak, at our side, yet also at the right hand of the Father, as Scripture portrays it, praying effectively even when our prayers are feeble, formal or half-hearted. There is another sense that we are never alone in this enterprise, and that lies in the truth that even when we are physically alone we are always caught up in the communal prayer of the Church, and this chapter will end with some thoughts about that.

But we must turn now to *how* we pray. During my lifetime there has been a wonderful recovery in spontaneity and freedom in how people pray. Fifty years ago, when people were taught to pray they were often given little books of prayer that provided them with set texts for use morning and evening. Sometimes these prayers were used so often that they were entirely committed to memory, and so the books were no longer necessary; but the prayers were unchanging because the texts were recited from memory. People may have known that ideally they could move beyond the texts, using them as a springboard into their own words or their own deep prayerful silences. But for many prayer remained a formal exercise ('saying my prayers'), like a little private liturgy at home, and did not venture beyond that.

In the last two generations, more people have learned that although texts and memory have their place, prayer at its best is something quite different. Sometimes it can be characterized as conversation. Not many of us have the kind of direct conversation with God that the Bible relates, for instance, in the description of the call of Samuel, who in the darkness of the night hears God calling him. He eventually responds, 'Speak, Lord, for your servant is listening,' and then receives a very clear message about the future – see 1 Samuel 3.1–15 for the whole story. But we have a sense that we can talk to God, whether out loud or silently, whether our lips move or not, in much the same way that we might talk to a lover, a parent or a friend; and we have a sense that God is speaking to us, as thoughts that do not feel as if they are our own come into our mind and heart. Because it is conversation rather than prepared speech, we do not quite know, when it begins, where it will be going. There can be a twist to the conversation, a surprise, sometimes the receiving of un-expected insight. Prayer as a kind of conversation is a good way to draw near to God.

If conversation is to have real quality, and go quite deep, it needs, of course, to come out of committed relationship. For we want to engage with God as lover, parent or friend, not as stranger or distant acquaintance. Relationship is the key. Before we can converse with God at any depth, there needs to be love and trust. This is something we have to work at; although even as we begin to open up to God, lovingly and trustingly, we find ourselves encountering one whose love and trust in us is already in place and who desires this deeper relationship with us. This is where the work of the Spirit is key, opening us to God, drawing us into relationship.

Where that love and trust are in place, we have the confidence to be honest in our praying. It is very easy, even when we think that we are praying from the heart, to say to God the things we believe God wants to hear: to praise God even though deep down we may be angry with him, or to give thanks for good things even though we have had a dreadful day that has left us wretched and tired. But God, who knows us better than we know ourselves, does not want us to try to fool him with beautiful pieties; he wants to allow us to know that he sees us as we really are. Sorrow, confusion, anger, inner turmoil and lament are all emotions we need to bring to the surface in honest prayer. Only when we do this can the healing touch of God begin to sort these emotions out and move us back into grace and peace. The model for such prayer is Jesus himself, in the Garden of Gethsemane before his arrest and his trial. The evangelist Luke describes it in this way in his Gospel:

> He withdrew from them about a stone's throw, knelt down, and prayed, 'Father, if you are willing, remove this cup from me; yet, not my will but yours be done.' Then an angel from heaven appeared to him and gave him strength. In his anguish, he prayed more earnestly, and his sweat became like great drops of blood falling down on the ground.
>
> (Luke 22.41–44)

Here is honest, vulnerable prayer, struggling for the right words, hiding nothing – as if one could – from a God who can see into the innermost thoughts and feelings of the heart.

Conversation and relationship are both important if prayer is to have authenticity. But the conversation will get us only so far. Paul, remember, in Romans 8, speaks of intercession where sighs take over, because words cannot go deep enough. We know it in our human relationships. Faltering, stilted words with a stranger might give way to articulate pouring out of words to a lover or a friend, but when things go deeper the words are suddenly difficult again, or inadequate, and we leave them behind, expressing relationship instead in easy silence together or in touch that has a sacramental quality. When we have reached that point in human relationship – with a friend it may be through an embrace, with a lover it may be through sexual intimacy, actions that convey what words fail to express – the experience has moved from conversation to communion. In our relationship with God, the experience of touch cannot be quite the same, though sometimes we can sense his kiss, his embrace, can feel ourselves enfolded; and in the Eucharist, which is a form of prayer whatever else it is, we can 'taste that the Lord is good'. But certainly with God we can come to that moment where all words fall away, and to be silent in his presence, attentive but at ease, is a deeper form of prayer. That is where we are wanting to be, where prayer has turned into loving communion with God. And sometimes, please God, we get there, even if fleetingly.

For me those three words – conversation, relationship, communion – remain key in entering a world of prayer. Other people have been helped by the acronym ACTS, standing for Adoration, Confession, Thanksgiving and Supplication. That sometimes sounds a bit neat to me, especially if these four elements of prayer are supposed to come in the right order. Conversation, let alone communion, is never quite as tidy as this; things emerge in just the order they tumble out. Sometimes, as in a human conversation, confession comes first because there is something big that needs sorting out. Sometimes thanksgiving may come first because there is huge gratitude in your heart for something wonderful that has happened. Sometimes there is such a need – for you, for somebody else or for God's world – that supplication or intercession, pleading with God, is where you have to begin. Honest encounter is not over-organized.

Nevertheless, there is something important to be learned from ACTS. Prayer does need the different elements, and they need to be in some sort of balance. If I have a friend of whom I am always asking help, but I never take the trouble to tell her how much I value our friendship, to say sorry for the occasions I don't have much time for her, or to thank her for many kindnesses, although she may go on giving the help I keep asking for, our relationship will not go deeper; through my neglect and selfishness it might die, to her great sadness. Prayer needs time to be given to expressing worship, love and trust. It needs realism about our failure and sin, and space to know myself forgiven and reconciled. It needs gratitude to the most generous of all lovers, parents and friends. It needs all those things, alongside the prayers for the needs of others and ourselves that God delights to receive. Adoration, confession, thanksgiving and supplication do all have their place.

Prayer also requires dedicated time and space. In terms of time, anyone serious about prayer needs to establish their primary prayer time of the day. There is no right or wrong as to when that is. Traditionally first thing on waking and last thing before sleep have been thought particularly appropriate, but that probably works only for those who live alone, and for some first thing and last thing may both be times when they are half-asleep! The appropriate time will vary according to our personality and our body clock and will change through the different stages of our life. One thing, however, is fairly certain. There does need to be a regular prayer time, so that it becomes deeply established in the rhythm of our day.

Place is almost as important as time. Most people will benefit from having a space into which they can retreat to pray. Some will slip into a church. If only more would do; then churches would indeed be the 'houses of prayer' we claim they are. Some people will want to be in the open air. For all the dangers that they may end up communing with creation but do not quite get in touch with the Creator, holy ground is not necessarily consecrated ground. Jacob, in Genesis 28, discovering at Bethel that the Lord was in that place, though he had not realized it, exclaimed, 'This is none other than the house of God, and this is the gate of heaven.' Moses, in Exodus 3.1–6, meeting God in the burning bush, took off his sandals, understanding that the place on which he stood was holy ground. For most of us that place will be a corner in our own home, somewhere that for all its ordinariness becomes the place where we meet God and rest in him: our own holy ground, a gate to heaven. We may furnish it with a candle or a cross or an icon. We may keep our Bible there, as a sign of the presence of the Christ who welcomes us and prays alongside us when we come into that space to talk with God or to be silent in his embrace.

Variety of posture may also be important for prayer. Sometimes I regret the loss of the invitation in the old Prayer Book to pray 'meekly kneeling upon your knees'. Whether in public liturgy or personal prayer, in kneeling rather less we have deprived ourselves of a particular experience of relationship with God, whereby we come to him humble, empty and expressing our total reliance on his goodness and mercy. Kneeling to pray, when we are physically able to do so, and even more, prostrating ourselves, may strengthen helpfully our dependence on God. But if we were always to pray kneeling, other aspects of our relationship with God might be neglected. To stand to pray is to express something of our sense of being grown-up, confident sons and daughters of God. God counts us worthy to stand in his presence to worship him. Always he is lifting us up off our knees and inviting us into a relationship more about love and friendship than about servile dependence. And sometimes to sit is the best posture for prayer – a gentle and open waiting upon the Lord, resting in him. All that really matters is that we should find which postures, as much as which times and places, enable us to meet with God and to find ourselves deepening our experience of his attention to us.

Most people need stimuli to lead them into prayer. Few of us, even when we want to open ourselves to the Spirit, can tune in to God instantly without some help. The stimulus may be an artefact, something that reflects the beauty of nature or the tradition of religious art. Prayer before a cross or crucifix, far from being a kind of idolatry, will enable many to picture Jesus and through that image to be drawn into the sense of the presence of God. Icons, candles or a Bible lying open may all serve the same purpose. Some people find it helpful to wrap themselves in a prayer shawl, being able to sense the warmth of the God who enfolds them in his love – and perhaps also the love of the person who made the shawl or gave it as a gift of friendship.

But for others the stimulus will be in what they hear, or do not hear. There is something profound and filled with God in a deep silence – the 'still small voice', as the King James Bible puts it, that Elijah encountered in 1 Kings.

> Now there was a great wind, so strong that it was splitting mountains
> and breaking rocks in pieces before the LORD, but the LORD was not
> in the wind; and after the wind an earthquake, but the LORD was
> not in the earthquake; and after the earthquake a fire, but the LORD
> was not in the fire; and after the fire a sound of sheer silence. When
> Elijah heard it, he wrapped his face in his mantle.
>
> (1 Kings 19.11–13)

In a world where there is so much noise, finding God may involve
shutting out all the sounds that distract and seeking the sheer silence
that is a kind of language of its own. It is a silence we do not look
immediately to fill. The very silence is a gift to explore, even though
for those of us who live busy, noisy lives this exploration into silence
can make us feel naked and exposed. Such vulnerability may bring
us closer to the God who clothes us in his love.

At other times the stimulus might not be silence but music, though
the two are not far removed from one another; the mystic John of
the Cross wrote of the 'silent music' of God's praise. In the language
of poetry we might speak of hearing in the silence the gentle song
of the angels. More often the music will be recorded, played on our
CD player or iPod and chosen because it helps draw us into a sense
of God's presence and the worship of heaven.

Recorded music has its place, whether or not it is intentionally
'sacred', but music in the heart might sometimes become music on
the lips. Augustine of Hippo is credited with the saying that 'the one
who sings prays twice', and song does indeed add a second dimension
to prayer. We are accustomed to singing together in church, and some
of us will break into the occasional tune as we go about our daily
work, but it is quite a different art, and a much neglected one, to
sing intentionally to God when we are on our own during a time
of prayer. But it is a way of being in tune with heaven and we do
not even need to be afraid that our singing is not very beautiful, for
if it is singing to honour him and to draw close to him, it will be
beautiful to God.

For all that visual and aural elements play their part, the stimulus
to prayer will often be words. We may have left behind an era where
personal praying often did not go beyond reciting words, but we still
need words other than our own to lead us into that mental and
spiritual space where we connect with God. There are at least three
sorts of word stimulus that can help us.

22

The first is Scripture. Because the Bible is where we find the word of God for us, we frequently need to let it lead us into prayer. Without it the words we think we hear in our prayer may be simply our talking to ourselves. But if we begin with the Scriptures an objective voice is addressing us, speaking into our situation, sometimes to challenge, sometimes to reassure. The Gospels particularly, wherein we encounter Jesus Christ, must often be the springboard into prayer, praying with the Jesus whom we have encountered as we open ourselves to the gospel message. It is not only in public liturgical readings of the Gospel that we can find ourselves conscious of the presence of the Lord. From the pages of the Scriptures we can sense his coming to us, and sometimes his voice is very clear.

The second sort of word stimulus is the liturgy. You cannot divorce personal prayer from corporate worship. To public worship we need to bring all that we have learned about prayer, so that we may make the liturgy prayerful. But, conversely, we should see our personal praying as an extension of the corporate worship in which we share, and draw into it whatever is helpful from the liturgical words the Church has given us to worship together. They are no substitute for the spontaneous praying of the heart, but they are frequently texts that lead us to the moment of connection where such praying can take over.

The implication of this is that memory is important in prayer. We do not much want little books open in our prayer space so that we can read liturgical texts, nor do we want to look them up on the computer and read them on screen. But we want to build up a memory bank of liturgical prayer, learned over the years, that can flow into our mind with hardly a conscious thought. For the liturgy, this means that there is a limit to the amount of variety of text that is profitable for us, otherwise we never get sufficient repetition to commit texts to memory. For ourselves, it might sometimes mean consciously learning a text that we have found striking or beautiful, in much the same way as our forebears used to learn the collect of the week, intentionally so that they were always accruing interest in the memory bank. To be honest, when, as is inevitable, there are days or even weeks when the more spontaneous prayer of the heart simply doesn't come, these texts are what get us through, keeping us to the discipline of prayer even when our heart is only half in it.

There is a third source of word stimulus – the spiritual and theological writers of the Christian tradition, especially those immensely creative, prayerful theologians of the patristic age (the 'fathers', though there are 'mothers' too), the holy men and women of other religious traditions, and poets of every age including our own. They all can lead us to the point of connectedness with God.

'But does God answer prayer?' For many that is a crucial question. All that I have written assumes that God is attentive to us, knows what it is we want to share with him before ever we articulate it, and engages with us. God answers in the sense that out of our commitment to prayer comes a deeper understanding of his purposes for us. God answers us in the sense that we are given some insight, however small, into his mind and heart. But does God answer in the sense of changing his mind, being persuaded? There is much in the Scriptures, especially in the Old Testament, that suggests that God is of a sort who can be persuaded. One delightful story that reveals a God who can be won round is Abraham's gentle persuasion that God should not stick to his intention to destroy the whole city of Sodom because of its wickedness, as told in Genesis 18. Abraham asks whether the city might be saved if there were just 50 righteous people within it. Yes, if there were 50, God would forgive the whole place for the sake of the 50. If there were 45? Yes, God would forgive if there were 45. If there were 40? Yes, if there were 40. Suppose there were 30? Yes, if there were 30. What if there were 20? Yes, if there were 20.

> Then [Abraham] said, 'Oh do not let the Lord be angry if I speak just once more. Suppose ten are found there.' He answered, 'For the sake of ten I will not destroy it.' And the LORD went his way, when he had finished speaking to Abraham. (Genesis 18.32–33)

Even here, I am not sure that we are witnessing God changing his mind, but God revealing, little by little, his true character and showing us the love and compassion by which he holds the world in being. The Old Testament is an uneven series of books. Sometimes for chapter after chapter there is no sign of that loving and compassionate God. We make God in our image and put on him the anger and need to punish and for retribution that sometimes overwhelm us. But if God is perfect love, absolute justice and all compassion, then his eternal and constant desire is always the well-being of his creation and of the human race he loves. In my prayer I do not need to change his mind – as if I were ever more in tune with the world's needs than he is. In intercession, and indeed in prayer for myself, I need to do only three things.

First I need to pour out to God my passion, concern and longing, so that, listening for his response, I may learn where I am in solidarity with God's will and where I am mistaken, and so conform myself to that will.

Second, I need to offer God that passion, concern and longing, so that it is caught up in and becomes a part of his own passion, concern and longing that keep the universe in being.

Third, I need to discover, through prayer that is sometimes a struggle, what particular thing I must do in any particular situation to bring about what God is intending for his creation and his children. Sometimes the answer is simply to go on praying, but on occasions God will show me that I can make a difference in some other way. I am sometimes myself the answer to my prayer. Such is true intercession.

That does not mean, of course, that everything that happens in this world is the will of God. As I have written already, human free will, leading into sin, often brings dreadful calamity into the world. Nor does it mean that we shall always be able to make sense of what God seems to be doing. The purposes of God, however consistently good they are, sometimes lie hidden in perplexing mystery, where only faith, kept alive in the darkness, will get us through. But even when it is like that, prayer is where we can find the grace to keep connected and to trust.

I have written of prayer as a deeply personal encounter with God, and it must be so, but it is never exactly 'private prayer'. No prayer is private; all prayer is corporate. Whenever we pray we do it in solidarity with the Church. We are always praying as part of a great company, across the world and across the centuries. When our own prayer is weak and feeble, this can be an impetus to keep praying, and also a source of encouragement that we are being carried along by something reliable, strong and immense. Although the way we pray may be not be the same as that of our neighbour and the texts we turn to for stimulus different, we are part of a community of prayer. I am always pleased to be somewhere where the church bell is rung morning and evening, not so much to summon people to the church to pray (though that is good), but simply to remind them that prayer is happening and that their own praying can be caught up in something bigger. For much the same reason I am glad when people draw into their prayers elements they know they share with others. For their Bible reading they may read one of the passages the Church provides for that particular day, so we are reading and exploring the same Scriptures. They may use each morning the Song of Zechariah (Benedictus), which is the gospel canticle in the Church's liturgical Morning Prayer, and each evening the Song of Mary (Magnificat), the gospel canticle at Evening Prayer. At the very least the use of the 'Our Father', the Lord's Prayer, links us with those across the world who share in this vast community of prayer. We need never feel alone when we pray.

One of the welcome recoveries of recent years has been a common shape and structure to the Church's liturgical daily prayer – Morning Prayer, Evening Prayer, Prayer During the Day and Night Prayer – in a rich but very flexible form that allows an increasing number of people to share in it at the level appropriate to them. In the Church of England, *Common Worship: Daily Prayer* represents the mainstream way forward, but it comes out of the same liturgical rethinking of the 'divine office', as it is traditionally called, as the Roman Breviary, the Taizé Office Book and other versions of liturgical daily prayer. The flexibility allows the same basic forms to be used both by those who gather physically in a community and equally by individuals who, physically alone, sense that they are caught up in a spiritual communal endeavour. It allows for full, rich, highly liturgical worship, yet is appropriate for those who are looking for a simple structure, with just a few texts and a lot of space for freedom, variety, spontaneity and perhaps more silence than words. It will be a wonderful blessing to the Church to develop a growing sense that all Christians, when they pray, consciously imagine themselves to be sharing in the daily prayer of one worldwide community.

And that community is more even than an international prayer partnership. Prayers on earth unite with the prayers of the saints and clock into the worship of heaven. The final chapter of this book will return to that mind-blowing truth. Sufficient to say here that the community of prayer knows no bounds.

Working with the Holy Spirit to connect with God in prayer can involve both discipline and struggle. Sometimes it is like a journey through a desert in search of water. But for all that – perhaps because of all that – it is sometimes a wonderful experience of sheer grace, joy and blessing, with an overwhelming sense of being drawn into the embrace of a loving God who always gives his whole self.

3

I believe in transforming worship

Prayer and worship are inextricably linked. Both are activities that, though we engage in them with a sense of solidarity with the wider community of prayer, can be done when no one else is in sight. Worship is the offering to God of praise, glory and honour in reverence and in love. It is something that can be done in community or distanced from community, in church or in a thousand other contexts.

But what is liturgy? Worship and liturgy are not exactly the same thing – although liturgy that has no worship in it is a cold and unsatisfactory activity.

Liturgy is that subtle blend of word, song, movement, gesture and silence that enables the people of God to worship together. Liturgy is, at a certain level, always about compromise, for it is concerned with finding forms that will enable people to experience something satisfying collectively. In that sense perhaps heaven will be a divine compromise, for that too will provide a setting where people with their infinite variety of personality and preference can experience something overwhelmingly wonderful that binds and draws together. You can worship without liturgy on your own. You can worship without church on your own. But the moment you engage in worship with others, there has to be a shared form, and that is where liturgy comes in. For that form is likely to be shaped by words, by music, by movement, by gesture and by silence. That is what liturgy is – the way in to the Church's corporate worship of God, the Father of our Lord Jesus Christ.

My starting point in reflecting how liturgical worship can touch people deeply and transform them is that evocative account of the call of the prophet Isaiah (Isaiah 6). This passage matters to me a great deal and has been deeply formative for me.

In the year that King Uzziah died, I saw the Lord sitting on a throne, high and lofty; and the hem of his robe filled the temple.

(Isaiah 6.1)

Isaiah is in the temple, sharing in worship, and so caught up does he become in this earthly, liturgical worship that he is transported, so to speak, to the heavenly places and finds himself drawn into the worship and indeed the conversation of heaven. It is a powerful passage, exciting because it shows us what liturgical worship at its very best can do, wonderful because it holds out to us the possibility of being joined to heaven.

Five truths emerge for me. First, I am reminded of the unutterable beauty, the sheer loveliness and the awesome holiness of God: 'Holy, holy, holy is the LORD of hosts; the whole earth is full of his glory,' the seraphs call to one another (Isaiah 6.3). We sell people short in the liturgy if we do not present them with this amazing God, clothed in beauty, loveliness and holiness: the one who first brings us to our knees and reduces us to silence, even if conversation then follows. Our liturgy sometimes lacks that sense of overwhelming. I believe it does so at our peril.

Second, the worship of the earth is raised to heaven. 'Grasping the heel of heaven' is a phrase I've often used to describe what our worship ought to be, and in this passage Isaiah has certainly done that; although in the Christian experience, of course, always as one stretches up there is a hand coming down to help to draw us into the divine presence. It is not just that we need to recover a sense of the divine, for that might be something that seems very remote, unattainable by us. But this passage gives us a sense that we are raised up, so that we are there, drawn right into the heart of it all. For a while we are part of the worship around the throne, as really there as the angels, as close as close can be to the God whom they worship. Christian worship has to yearn to be that, drawn for a while into the experience of heaven.

Third, there is a message about guilt and cleansing.

I said, 'Woe is me! I am lost, for I am a man of unclean lips, and I live among a people of unclean lips; yet my eyes have seen the King, the LORD of hosts!'
Then one of the seraphs flew to me, holding a live coal that had been taken from the altar with a pair of tongs. The seraph touched my

mouth with it and said: 'Now that this has touched your lips, your guilt has departed and your sin is blotted out.' (Isaiah 6.5–7)

. Christians have tended recently to sit rather lighter than in the past to confession and absolution in worship, and perhaps there is a need for something of a rebalancing. But it has been an Anglican insight, expressed in the Introduction to Morning and Evening Prayer in the Book of Common Prayer, that penitence should always form part of public liturgy. And if we are serious about liturgy that celebrates the holiness of God, it follows naturally, for that is the only possible first response to sheer holiness. 'Woe is me! I am lost!' is a serious recognition that the light of God shows up the shoddiness and ugliness that is part of us. Liturgy needs to recognize this, and to provide both space and language to give it expression and to celebrate the joy of forgiveness and reconciliation – 'your guilt has departed and your sin is blotted out'.

Fourth, out of the vision of God comes not only a sense of unworthiness (though that must come first) but also a sense of vocation: 'Then I heard the voice of the Lord, saying, "Whom shall I send, and who will go for us?" And I said, "Here am I; send me!"' (Isaiah 6.8).

I do not doubt that God has many ways of helping people to recognize what he is calling them to. There is no single way in which vocation is discovered and discerned. But I am clear that what happened to Isaiah is and can be experienced by other people. It happened to me. It is a significant pattern: while sharing in the liturgy, participating in worship, you find yourself drawn close to God; you recognize your unworthiness but experience the forgiveness of God, and then offer to God your life. If there is good liturgy, more and more people will sense the calling of God to whatever it is he wants them to do with the rest of their lives.

Fifth, worship leads to mission. They are the two great privileges God lays upon his Church – to offer him worship (worship that he always turns into blessing) and to share his mission. But what Isaiah's experience underlines for us is that these are not two entirely distinct activities; the one leads into the other. Good liturgy is the springboard of effective mission. Effective mission emerges from the vision of God's holiness and the sense of vocation – sharing his work – that follows.

I have written extensively about liturgical worship and I only summarize here material that can be found elsewhere. But Isaiah 6 leads us straight to a fundamental affirmation that liturgy is meant for worship before it is meant for anything else. Other good things happen when Christians gather to celebrate the liturgy, but worship needs to be what really counts. It is this grasping of the heel of heaven that matters, wanting above all else to be in communion with God, singing his praises, offering to him our prayers and sensing ourselves touched by his holiness. My worry in the life of the Church is not so much that it does not always happen, but that for many there is little expectation that it will ever happen. It is simply not on their agenda. We need to cultivate expectation and yearning and not let people settle for something less.

Much else does indeed happen in the liturgy as well as worship. There can be good teaching. There can be deep fellowship. There can be powerful conversion experiences. But these are the gift of God, for it is in God's nature to take what we offer and turn it into a gift, to transform it. Of course, we see this most strikingly in the Eucharist; we bring bread and wine to the altar, but when God has touched them by his Spirit we receive them back, now a gift to us, changed, transformed, now for us the body and blood of Christ. That's what the transforming God does. He does it with human lives also. And he does it with the worship we offer and so makes the liturgy a setting in which he can make himself known, touch people deeply, draw them into community and bring about transformation.

For this to happen there needs to be on our part a real openness to the Spirit; as the last chapter sought to show, that means a prayerfulness that will give the liturgy both life and depth. Put very simply, what we need to do with the liturgy is to pray it. We need to bring to its celebration all that we have learned about prayer and plant this firmly in the liturgy, thus making it a setting in which God can and will act to transform. At some points in the liturgy it is very clear that what the assembly is doing is indeed praying – times of silence, confession, intercession and thanksgiving, worshipful singing. But those moments of overt intentional prayer need to create a kind of rhythm of prayer that carries on as a sort of undercurrent to the liturgy, while we do the other things – listening to the Scriptures, engaging with the sermon, greeting one another at the kiss of peace, and at the Eucharist breaking the bread and gathering around the table to receive the life that Jesus offers.

For me all liturgical worship – linking us to heaven, providing the setting for transformation in our lives and in the Church and maybe as a model for transformation in society, drawing us into communal praying – is at the heart of Christian life and discipleship. These things can and do happen, in settings large and small, sacramental and non-sacramental, formal and informal. They can happen in the daily and weekly round of liturgical observance, in the occasional pastoral offices and in the community celebrations that draw people in from the fringe of the Church on popular festivals and feast days. On none of these occasions should we looking for less.

Nevertheless, for me the ultimate place of liturgical formation and transformation is the Eucharist, on which I concentrate for the rest of this chapter. In my experience the Eucharist is where so much more than bread and wine can be changed. I want Jesus Christ to be at the heart of my life, and my Christian pilgrimage has taught me that the Eucharist is the setting where that can be brought about effectively, though little by little. Every Eucharist has the potential to be a moment of grace. And, unconsciously most of the time, of course, I sense that the gift of Christ in the Eucharist is an important element in what energizes me for my ministry and for my part in the mission of God and of the Church, both as a human being and as a priest.

I sometimes find myself singing Francis Stanfield's Victorian hymn 'Sweet sacrament divine', the Catholic worship song of its day. At a certain emotional level I warm to it, not least because of Stanfield's evocative tune he composed for it. But in the end he's got it wrong for me. The Eucharist and the sacramental presence are not 'where restless yearnings cease', nor are they 'the ark from the ocean's roar' and 'the shelter blest'. They are where the Spirit animates, motivates and energizes, makes things come alive, renews me for ministry, mission and the enjoyment of life. Not so much sweet sacrament of peace or rest, but sacrament of life.

I want to explore six truths about the Eucharist.

The first is that the Eucharist draws me into an experience of the reality of God. It is good that the Eucharist is accessible, that it can (and ought to) be welcoming, hospitable and full of delightful fellowship; but it is also an awesome encounter with the living God, who is, as I have said already, holiness beyond our understanding, mystery beyond our comprehension, beauty beyond our imagining, love beyond our measuring. When we lose sight of that, or at least of the potential of experiencing that just occasionally, we have walked away from a stupendous truth that can form us and transform us. Our feet on the ground, we nevertheless stretch up to catch hold of heaven, to participate albeit fleetingly in the worship of the angels and the saints. The way we celebrate the Eucharist needs to take that into account. It needs poetry, beauty, longing prayerfulness and deep silences, if we are to experience something of heaven. We need it not just for its own sake but because it is the sheer holiness, the sense of being overwhelmed by the reality of God, that will motivate us, as Isaiah found, into mission. Only if I have caught the vision of God will I be motivated to share the mission of God.

John Wesley spoke of the sacrament of the Lord's Supper as a 'converting ordinance'. God has many ways of bringing people to faith, quite a lot of them entirely outside the liturgical context, and quite a few outside the Church! But one of his ways is to draw them into liturgy that sweeps them off their feet; they sense the reality of the divine presence – supremely in the Eucharist – which picks them up, shakes them, and puts them down in another place. No one has spoken a word to them, there has been no teaching or explanation. Worship has revealed to them a new reality they had not seen before. That's what the Eucharist can do. It is profoundly missional.

The second truth is that the Eucharist is an extension of the Incarnation. I suppose this is the truth to which the reservation of the sacrament most obviously points. There in the aumbry, the tabernacle, the pyx or the sacrament house, is what to the world's eye at least is bread or wafer, yet I experience it as the dwelling place of Christ. The God who became flesh and blood in Jesus his Son is the God who created matter, who hides in the material, is clothed in the physical and pours out his grace in the sacramental. This is the God who loves his creation, everything that he has made and seen to be good, and as part of that – the summit of that – the human race, for whom his love goes deeper still. The truth is that the sacramental, material, physical, incarnational presence we focus in the bread of the Eucharist fills the universe and makes itself, Godself, available to all who will receive it. The sacrament is always a reminder of a God who loves the world and yearns for it to respond to its Creator.

I suppose that it has been the insight of the catholic movement in the Church, which has helped to form me as the kind of Christian I am, that does not let the cross so take over the Eucharist that the crib is forgotten. Every Eucharist is a reclaiming of the sacrifice of Calvary, but every Eucharist is also a reclaiming of Bethlehem. There is a striking passage in a famous rallying speech by Bishop Frank Weston of Zanzibar at the 1923 Anglo-Catholic Congress. Weston speaks of the 'Christ of Bethlehem', the one God sent as the supreme manifestation of a God at work in the material and the physical. Weston said this:

> I recall you and myself to him, and I want you first to listen to the call of the Christ of Bethlehem, eternal God made man for you, made man for me, Jesus the babe of Bethlehem. I want you to listen to him as he leaps from the Father's throne across the gulf that separates the Creator from creation, across the gulf that separates holiness from sin. Listen to him as he leaps that gulf and appears in human form amongst us men. Listen to him as he speaks to you: 'By this shall all men know that ye are my disciples if ye have love one to the other'. I recall you to the Christ of Bethlehem.

You have to forgive the gender-exclusive language of the time, but for me Weston describes a wonderful extension of the Incarnation. For all the uniqueness of the presence of God in the man Jesus Christ, there is a life-giving extension of that in the presence in the sacrament of the Eucharist, where we speak of the Lord's body and blood, and indeed in all sacramental acts. For the matter is sometimes bread and sometimes water and sometimes oil, and the matter, the material, is also sometimes – equally physical – the human hand, the embrace, the kiss. All this I learn from reflecting on the mystery of how God takes the bread and wine that we place upon an altar table, and by the operation of the Holy Spirit inhabits that bread and wine in a way that is more than symbol as we give thanks, break and share; and God continues to be present in a real sense beyond the celebration in the bread we keep as a focus for our prayers. And, if this is not to jump too easily on a fashionable bandwagon, I do believe this emphasis on the God of the physical and material helps us to see that part of our mission, which is his mission, is to care for our environment, to sustain this planet. The God who inhabits bread and wine yearns for the whole creation to be drawn to him and to respond to him.

The third truth is this. The Eucharist reveals to me the depths of God's love. That is so because the Eucharist always faces me with the cross. Every time we celebrate the Eucharist, even on Christmas Day, even on Easter Day, even at Pentecost, the Eucharist proclaims the cross: Christ's 'death until he comes'. I confess that I find it very difficult to unscramble doctrines of the atonement, but I know that when I look upon the crucifix I see wonderful sacrificial, compassionate love and know it to be a revelation of the nature of God himself. And when on the altar at the Eucharist I look upon the bread and the cup, or take them into my hands, there too I see a wonderful sacrificial, compassionate love and know it to be a revelation of the nature of God himself: the wine in the cup because the precious blood is shed, drained away for the life of the world, and all for love, and bread because the bread is broken, for the body of the Lord was broken, and all for love. Only the broken body could redeem. What needs to be received into our hands is not some beautiful, aesthetically pleasing, rounded host, but broken bread, ragged, jagged, always showing me the cost of divine loving. And I want that lovely yet disturbing truth to provide for me the impetus to loving, to help me embrace a vocation where a compassionate loving draws me into collaborative mission with a God who loves his creation with a passion I can hardly begin to emulate.

The Eucharist gives me an insight into the depths of God's love in another way: it holds before me the picture of the Trinitarian God. The much represented icon of the hospitality of Abraham by Andrei Rublev, with its three figures sitting, eating and seemingly inviting another to join them, says something about a Trinity who beckons us in to share the divine life. It is a powerful image. The eucharistic celebration is always a Trinitarian event. We look up to the Father and we ask him to send the Holy Spirit to make the bread and the wine the body and blood of Christ the Son. And we look up to the Father and we ask him to send the Holy Spirit to make us also the body of Christ the Son. Trinitarian activity, loving relationship, almost, so to speak, acted out before our very eyes. And we do that, and God does that, entirely so that we may be drawn to the love feast, nourished by the divine food and the divine life. Nourishment that is the joy of feasting, but also equipping for ministry and mission, sustenance for living out faith in the world of every day.

Fourth, the Eucharist brings the world to God through the intercession of God's people. Of course, God upholds the world every moment of its existence, or it would cease to be. His loving care for it is not dependent on us. But it is a delightful part of the divine providence that his care for the world is expressed in his response to our prayers of offering and intercession. In the Eucharist, where intercession should never be narrow, but always a holding up to God of the immensity of creation – the world in all its joy and pain, the human race in all its diversity – we offer it to him that he may bless and transform. Sometimes we bring that identifying with the divine will, joining our longings with the divine longings, into the eucharistic prayer itself, so that the world becomes part of what we offer, in union with Christ and his sacrifice, alongside our own souls and bodies and our more specific intentions.

I have long been inspired by the opening sentences of Pierre Teilhard de Chardin's 'Mass on the world', which I first read 40 years ago. The words still move me. Father Pierre is on a scientific expedition, away from church and sacramental life, but he is a priest.

> Since once again, Lord, I have neither bread, nor wine, nor altar, I will raise myself beyond these symbols, up to the pure majesty of the real itself; I, your priest, will make the whole earth my altar and on it will offer you all the labours and sufferings of the world.
>
> Over there, on the horizon, the sun has just touched with light the outermost fringe of the eastern sky. Once again, beneath this moving sheet of fire, the living surface of the earth wakes and trembles, and once again begins its fearful travail. I will place on my paten, O God, the harvest to be won by this renewal of labour. Into my chalice I shall pour all the sap which is to be pressed out this day from the earth's fruits . . .
>
> One by one, Lord, I see and I love all those whom you have given me to sustain and charm my life . . . And again, one by one – more vaguely, it is true, yet all-inclusively – I call before me the whole vast anonymous army of living humanity; those who surround me and support me though I do not know them; those who come and those who go; above all, those who in office, laboratory and factory, through their vision of truth or despite their error, truly believe in the progress of earthly reality and who today will take up again their impassioned pursuit of the light . . .

Receive, O Lord, this all-embracing host which your whole creation,
moved by your magnetism, offers you at this dawn of a new day.
Pierre Teilhard de Chardin, in *Hymn of the Universe*

Teilhard de Chardin speaks in these terms despite having no bread,
no wine, no altar. But he speaks thus because as a Christian and a
priest he has been formed by the Eucharist, by the hundreds of times
he has had bread and wine and, taking them into his hands, has
sensed that he lifts up to God the whole creation and the entire
human race. The fact that so much intercession lacks this sense of
the cosmic and the global might easily blind us to the truth that in
relating the creation to the Creator through intercession, in the power
of the Spirit and in union with Christ, in lifting the creation to the
Father, we further the mission of God – which is, in part, to draw
everything through Christ to himself. Would that we could banish
wordy and banal intercession and capture this sense that what we
do is a deep engagement with the activity of God.

The fifth is that the Eucharist draws us in only to send us out.

I often regret that those who worked on the Church of England's
Common Worship Eucharist (I was one of them) named the final
section stage of the liturgy 'the Dismissal'. 'The Gathering' comes first,
then 'the Liturgy of the Word', then 'the Liturgy of the Sacrament',
and last 'the Dismissal'. You cannot avoid the impression that it is
a letting-down sort of word. 'The Sending out' would have been
stronger. For that is what happens at the end of the Eucharist. We
are sent out in the power of the Spirit, transformed by the activity of that same Spirit, to live and work to God's praise and glory.
The liturgists love to argue about how you can possibly translate satis-
factorily into English the last imperative of the Latin mass, *Ite, missa
est*. 'Go, the mass is ended' is a cop-out, for it avoids the relationship between *missa*, mission, dismissal and the whole emphasis on
sending. 'Go, be sent,' would be better. And from *missa* comes Mass;
it always delights my heart that among all the names we have for the
sacrament – Lord's supper, Holy Communion, breaking of the bread,
Eucharist, all of which point to a particular emphasis in relation to
the sacrament – there is one name, Mass, that takes me straight to the
end and reminds me that I come in to be nourished and equipped
only so that I may be sent out to live the Christian life and to engage
in Christian mission. And even if you are a contemplative able to

kneel for long periods before the blessed sacrament, if you really are engaged in communion with God in Christ, sooner or later, because you have been transformed, you will hear the imperative, 'Now go, this beauty you have encountered here, this love that has embraced you here, this sense of the divine that has captured you here, go and share it, join in my mission.'

The sixth and final truth is that the Eucharist is always a feast for the hungry and a setting for hospitality to the dispossessed. In that same speech in 1923 Bishop Weston famously declared:

> I say to you, and I say it to you with all the earnestness that I have, that if you are prepared to fight for the right of adoring Jesus in his blessed sacrament, then you have got to come out from before your tabernacle and walk, with Christ mystically present in you, out into the streets of this country, and find the same Jesus in the people in your cities and your villages. You cannot claim to worship Jesus in the tabernacle, if you do not pity Jesus in the slum . . . Go out into the highways and hedges where not even the bishops will try to hinder you. Go out and look for Jesus in the ragged, in the naked, in the oppressed and sweated, in those who have lost hope, in those who are struggling to make good. Look for Jesus. And when you see him, gird yourselves with his towel and try to wash their feet.

The Eucharist is *for* the poor, the ragged and the oppressed and *about* the poor, the ragged and the oppressed, for it celebrates a compassionate God and a vulnerable saviour. It is a feast where rank and status have no place, there are no front row seats for the wealthy, and no accolade for being the most smartly dressed. At least it should not be. At this table all are equal and the hungry are fed. The slums still exist, if not so much in our own country but in many lands; here, if we do not have slums we have those on the margins, the oppressed and the downtrodden. The feast is for them – the inclusive supper of the one who in an outpouring of love died for all. God's love, changing and transforming, is at work in the Eucharist to give those on the margins the dignity of being beloved sons and daughters and honoured guests.

Through all these truths and in all these ways I encounter Jesus Christ in the Eucharist. He is there among us, in the community that gathers, in the gospel that we proclaim and in the meal we share. Each encounter has the capacity to change and transform me. By the power of the Spirit, transforming worship can change the Church and hasten the kingdom. Jesus says to the woman at the well in John 4.24: 'God is spirit, and those who worship him must worship in spirit and truth.'

4

I believe in a mission-shaped Church

———◆•◆•◆———

I believe in a mission-shaped Church, but my fundamental instinct in relation to the Church is not so much to believe in her, but to love her, even when she seems at times less than lovable. The Church is built on the rock of faith, as Jesus assured Simon Peter, and the powers of hell will not defeat it. And Christ loves the Church, for all its frailty. When the Church drives me to distraction, I hold on to the teaching of the apostle Paul in Ephesians:

> Christ loved the church and gave himself up for her, in order to make her holy by cleansing her with the washing of water by the word, so as to present the church to himself in splendour, without a spot or wrinkle or anything of the kind – yes, so that she may be holy and without blemish. (Ephesians 5.25–27)

Christ loves the Church and so should Christians – not uncritically, but love her nonetheless. She is an instrument of God's mission and the task of the Christian, under the Spirit, is to make her more so.

Can we really talk about the Church as 'she'? Paul certainly does; he thinks of the Church as the bride of Christ. In some sentences the feminine sounds perfectly natural, as when Paul speaks of Christ loving her. At other times the Church feels more like an 'it'. But I have decided to write of the Church throughout this chapter as 'she', partly for consistency's sake, but also as a repeated reminder that the Church is beloved by Christ, like a bridegroom loves a bride, and that it is only by her relationship with him that she is able to flourish and reach her potential.

So what kind of Church are we talking about? I believe that we need to think both big and small. The Church is universal. Through our baptism we join a community that knows no barriers of language, nationality or ethnic origin. We join a community that encompasses

Christians who wear extraordinarily different labels, a community that has a hundred of ways of speaking of the truths of the gospel and a thousand ways of celebrating them. But the Church is not fundamentally the local parish or diocese or even a national church, let alone one of a series of networks of the like-minded. She is something much more exciting, much more challenging to live in, and in the end much more glorious: a community transcending both time and place.

But because she needs earthing in the particular, the Church is, at the same time, also local. Most of the time people cannot cope with the idea of a conceptual Church across the world. They need to earth their experience of the community of the baptized in brothers and sisters they can see, pray with, cooperate with, learn from and love. So the Church is just as genuinely the local community of faith in which each person lives out their discipleship. If we want to get the picture of what it is like to be the Church, we need to look at both the universal and the local and look for signs of growth in both.

So how can the Church, both universal and local, effectively be what God calls her to be? I find myself wanting to pick up and examine again an affirmation that we often take for granted, or even avoid because it can sound heavy. However, it is worth looking at afresh. It is part of the Creed of Nicaea, dating from the early fourth century and one of the foundation documents of the Church: the affirmation that 'we believe in one, holy, catholic and apostolic Church'. What might each of those four adjectives – one, holy, catholic and apostolic – mean in relation to the Church?

First, the Church is one. She has a deep and fundamental unity and she seeks to deepen that. Her unity, her 'oneness' in Jesus Christ, is set out beautifully in the high-priestly prayer of Jesus in John 17. Its basic plea is 'that they may be one'.

> I ask not only on behalf of these, but also on behalf of those who will believe in me through their word, that they may all be one. As you, Father, are in me and I am in you, may they also be in us, so that the world may believe that you have sent me.   (John 17.20–21)

Again there is the universal dimension. Jesus prays that they be one 'so that the world may believe'. What does it mean for us to want to be more truly one in order that the world may believe? It means sitting light to entrenched denominationalism, the historic divisions that divide and scar the body of Christ. Yet it also means affirming the theologians of the different churches who are trying to lay to rest the ghosts of old controversies and to find language that will enable people to discover that there is a greater unity in what they believe than they had understood to be the case.

I also believe that it means a generosity of attitude that does not always require our fellow Christians to see everything just as we do, but to recognize that there is more than one path through Christ to the Father.

All those things – sitting light to entrenched historical divisions, affirming those who work for a new common language, being generous to those of other traditions – then need to flow down from the universal to the more particular at a number of levels.

They need to flow down to the level of the Anglican Communion, where we are in danger of tearing ourselves apart over issues that, though important, ought not to deflect us from our fundamental task of giving glory to God and witness to his Son Jesus Christ in our world of despair. Tensions within the Communion have been inevitable, for the Communion is found living out the Christian gospel in such widely differing contexts. Perhaps the only way to hold together is through diocesan partnerships across cultures and theological divides. For this is where people can develop friendships in which individuals can speak the truth as they perceive it, listen with real attentiveness to others, learn to respect one another and to see the Communion as such a precious gift that holding it together becomes a primary objective. My own experience of that, in creating a partnership with an evangelical conservative diocese in Africa and a more catholic liberal diocese in America, has shown me that such committed relationships not only change perspectives but bring a far deeper sense of delight in being part of both the Communion and the universal Church.

Those same things – sitting light, affirming, being generous – need to flow down to the level of the local diocese or deanery or Churches Together grouping, where there can be suspicion, envy and the failure of charity. And then, finally, they need to flow down to the Church at her most local, in the congregation and the parish, where there has to be a real commitment to unity, to being one in order that the world may believe.

At all these levels, from the universal to the very local, it sometimes means living with a tension between the unity of the Church and the truth as we perceive it. Unity and truth sometimes seem to pull us in two directions and we simply have to hold that tension creatively and lovingly.

'Lovingly' is, in this context, a crucial and challenging word. Allowing the truth to be spoken without the loss of unity requires deep fellowship and real love. And, whether internationally or locally, deep fellowship and real love are hard work and need constant attention. But only real love can transform relationships so that unity and truth come together and the Church becomes united. This real love, for all the attention it requires, is divine gift. Indeed it is simply a reflection of divine being. God is love and that love is expressed in his very nature, in the loving in the Trinity, and in the loving that had Jesus praying through the enabling of the Spirit to the Father 'that they may all be one as we are one'. If the Church is to be true to her calling, she must be one, for God is one, and she must seek that oneness, that unity, through love, for God is love.

Second, the Church is holy. That means first of all that she is part of the divine providence. She is blessed by Jesus Christ, the one who loves her and gave himself for her, as Paul says. She is not a merely human organization. She is, as I understand it, a divine organism. An ancient prayer from the Gelasian Sacramentary calls her 'a wonderful and sacred mystery' – and so she is, on a good day! She is holy because God wills her to be.

She is holy also – and I think this is probably more important – because her motivation comes from her experience of the reality of God, the reality of his sheer holiness. Jesus is my friend, God is my companion, but alongside that sense of intimacy with the divine I have to keep before me that other element, the sheer beauty, overwhelming otherness, immense holiness of God. The Church is holy both because she seeks on earth to echo the worship of heaven and also because it is that vision of the sheer holiness of God that motivates her.

The holiness of the Church expresses itself in prayer – hands and hearts lifted to heaven in adoration, in penitence, in intercession, in longing, in love. It expresses itself when people come together, minds and voices joined with the angels and the saints, in authentic worship: joyful, yet in touch with pain, yearning for heaven, and sometimes moving beyond words and music into sheer silence. There is that wonderful verse in Revelation: 'There was silence in heaven for about half an hour' (Revelation 8.1). The singing stopped and they were still, knowing that God is God, knowing that God is real, that God is holy, holy, holy Lord. If the Church is to be the God-centred community, then prayer and worship, the activities that catch us up into the holiness, must be priorities.

Again, this has worldwide and local application. If we could recover a greater sense of the Church as a prayer partnership right across the world, would that not be an immense resource in God's mission? But more locally we need every church community to see itself as a network of prayer and those local communities in relation to one another. Yes, if the Church is to be the God-centred community, she must be holy, for God is holy.

Third, the Church is catholic. Of course, when we hear the word 'catholic' misunderstanding abounds. I use the word here in the same way as the Creed does, in its broadest and most inclusive way. In saying that the Church is catholic we mean that the Church is everywhere, universal, in all times and in all places. Church sometimes means the local group of Christians, but always within an understanding of the universality of the Church that knows no bounds of culture, nationality or tradition. To belong to something bigger than the Church as I encounter it locally is a huge encouragement – although it is also sometimes a constraint. I need to keep relatively in step with Christian brothers and sisters who do not seem to go at my speed or see things my way. It can also be a source of wonder and delight. Look, God is at work in them too!

Being one does not mean being uniform. The catholic community, with all her variety and local colour, even occasionally her eccentricity, is glorious in her diversity. And I think that in terms of the local Church it means a similar desire to avoid the monochrome. It would be good if every church were a church of many colours. Even in the local congregation, we should celebrate diversity and rejoice in the very differences that might otherwise divide.

If the Church is to be the God-centred community, she must be catholic in that broad sense of inclusive, diverse and everywhere. For God is a God who loves, includes, blesses all his children. God is a God who created the human race in its glorious diversity. God is a God who is everywhere. 'In him,' as Paul reminded the Athenians, 'we live and move and have our being' (Acts 17.28). All of us – not one culture, not one nation, not one religious tradition – all of us have our being in God. The God-centred community is catholic.

The Church is apostolic. That means, first of all, that she is rooted in the Christ experience, the experience that took hold of the apostles and changed them, making them bold in their testimony to the one they followed and to the events they witnessed. The apostolic community looks to Jesus as its founder, the one who knew what he wanted the Church to do and commanded her to go and teach and baptize all nations. She looks to Christ's death and resurrection and the imparting of the Spirit as the saving events that launched her into her mission.

Second, to be an apostolic community means being committed to proclaiming the message of the apostles, being loyal to the faith once delivered to the saints, wanting to share the good news of salvation, needing to tell and being innovative and adventurous in the telling. We may fail in that sometimes, universally or even locally, but, if we are an apostolic Church, proclaiming afresh the faith that gripped the apostles and poured out in their preaching, it is our vocation. We are like Peter in Jerusalem on the day of Pentecost and Paul in cities all over the then-known world.

And the Church is apostolic in the sense that it is the 'community of the sent'. Apostles do not stand still. Always they are on the move, looking for new places to proclaim the message, seeking new communities where the good news has not yet been heard, searching for people whom the Spirit of God has prepared to hear about Jesus and to receive him into their lives. A community of hope in a world of despair will be full of people with a divine sense of being sent, people with news to tell.

That too needs both its universal and its local application. It is wonderful to see the renewal in our own day of a sense of mission right across the Church, and as part of that a new confidence in evangelism. Renewal in a variety of forms has prepared the way. The early ecumenical movement, which broke down barriers between churches and allowed Christians to share insights and work together where previously they had worked apart or even in rivalry, paved the way. The rediscovery of the power of the Scriptures in the Roman Catholic Church after the Second Vatican Council also brought renewal. The liturgical movement, loosening up and renewing worship across the churches, has enabled us to recover some lost paths into contemplation, holiness, worship and prayer. The charismatic movement has breathed in new life, sometimes in very unexpected places and some mightily surprised people, and helped recognize afresh the Spirit's gifts, and its influence has reached far beyond the communities that would label themselves charismatics. All these forms of renewal have prepared the Church for what we now see coming into its own: a Church more seized by mission than for a long time.

There are pockets of resistance, of course, and people with their heads in the sand; but across the world, and certainly in our own nation, there is a new willingness to be bold and take risks so that we may have a 'mission-shaped church'. And that is just what an apostolic community is and what a God-centred community needs to be.

If the Church is to be the kind of Church God wants her to be, she needs to go on taking very seriously those four marks to which she has sought to be true through the ages. They are as relevant as ever, though we need to express them in fresh ways. The Church is one, holy, catholic and apostolic.

But, in a sense, everything I have written so far could have been said in every generation and is universal in its application. It has been, after all, an unpacking of a timeless Creed. But what about being a mission-shaped Church here in England in the twenty-first century?

There is a need to look again at what kind of Church we have to be to serve God's world and to share God's mission in that world. The conventional wisdom is that we should be a 'both . . . and . . . Church', what the Archbishop of Canterbury calls 'a mixed economy Church'. In other words, we need to have confidence in our heritage, using all the traditional tools at our disposal, having a sense of history and continuity and not severing links with the society around us. And we should do new things also, to be imaginative, creative and bold – 'fresh ways of being Church', as the current phrase goes. Much of this 'and' will be untidy, provisional and uncomfortable for some of us.

I believe in an untidy Church. In some ways it hurts me to say it, for most of my instincts are towards tidiness, but in the life of the Church today that is not helpful. I think God is a God of order, but that is not quite the same as a God of tidiness, and in any case I am clear that what God brings most fundamentally out of chaos is not order but life. And that is infinitely more important and more precious. When I say we want an untidy Church, I mean that there is no one solution to the challenges that face us. God wants to work with our communities as they are: with the people in our churches and communities with their particular aptitudes, gifts and foibles. God wants us to find out what is right in each particular situation and to go for it. Of course, in order to preserve our unity, our holiness, our catholicity and our apostolicity, we have to apply some limits, but not too many, lest we suppress the promptings of the Spirit. The pattern of ministry and mission appropriate for a grouping of rural parishes may be very different from that for a suburban deanery. The worship that will help older congregations in villages may be very different from that appropriate for a youth congregation. One deanery may know that it needs to fund an evangelist's post, another deanery a detached youth worker, another a chaplain in the local further education college, another a batch of priests ordained for specifically local ministry. The Church needs a culture of permission, where new things will spring up and some very old ones come back into fashion. The result will be a much less tidy Church – one more difficult for a bishop to hold together – but a Church in which the Spirit is moving and fresh shoots of growth appearing. It will be worth taking the risk, living with untidiness, pushing at the boundaries of church order, flourishing on dilemma. That is a bold thing for the Church to set out to do – to flourish on dilemma.

Yet we do not want an overstretched Church. I don't so much mean financially overstretched, for I believe that the money is there, waiting to be given if only people can catch the vision of what could be done for the sake of Christ and his gospel. I mean that we don't want clergy at breaking point. We don't want laity so busy being churchy in their house groups and their ministry teams that they have to opt out of the life of the wider communities in which they live and work. We don't want to be so involved in the Church that there is no one left to build up the kingdom.

So I believe in the 'both . . . and . . . but . . . Church'; the 'but' is the things that the Church can manage without, and that is the difficult part. Closing down the parish organization that we all know has had its day. Moving the funding from something quite important, but not crucial, to something even more important. Giving up on something you really value, when you are not sure you ought to do so, lest you have got it wrong. We need to seek discernment to know what we can let go of in order to be a slimmer, fitter Church; that might, sometimes, even mean letting go of the church building we've loved all our lives.

I dream of a Church that will have a lot of windows and many doors that are usually open; it will be a hospitable place to make coming in very easy, a place where acceptance will always be on offer. I dream of a Church that will know her distinctiveness as the body of the Lord Jesus Christ and will hold on to and share joyfully and passionately 'the sacred and imperishable proclamation of eternal salvation', as we read at the end of Mark's Gospel; yet this Church will always be in dialogue with the secular world, the local community, people of goodwill of many faiths and none, with those millions who seek for meaning but do not come to the Church, as she is, to find it. Dialogue is hard work. To engage in it effectively we need to be confident in our relationship with Christ, to know what we believe, to be equipped by the Holy Spirit to speak with conviction of the gospel we have embraced, and to listen with humility. We need to be a listening and a speaking Church; both have their part to play.

I also dream of a Church where some of it will be almost unrecognizable to me, even where some of it will seem very strange to me. We do not yet know where the 'fresh expressions' and 'emerging Church' movement will take us. Pioneering work is needed that goes far beyond creating alternative worship services in established congregations and church buildings. New forms of Church have to be allowed to develop without any assumption that they are a bridge into mainstream conventional Church. They may need to exist long term alongside, but only very loosely integrated into, the main body of the Church.

It is quite clear that there are lessons the mainstream Church can learn from some of the pioneering forms of church life. There is certainly something to learn from the 'cell church'. In many parts of the world (in South America, for instance) and in some of our largest churches in Britain, people are recognizing that there is real growth – for the individual spiritually and for the Church numerically – when the basic unit of Church life is the cell, a very small group of ten or a dozen who meet usually in homes and create the kind of trust and intimacy in which there can be real exploration of faith, support for one another and where even the shyest find their voice and grow in confidence. The cell, of course, grows, and then divides, and there are two cells. The congregations of some of our village churches are cell size, but they are cells operating in a large, cold, overfurnished building, worshipping and studying the faith in a style that almost precludes the trust and intimacy that leads to growth. There may be some important insights for the small congregation from the cell church; and for the larger congregation that has stopped growing, some key lessons about putting in place a level of church life where growing happens.

Then there's the network church. Geography has always mattered to the Church. People have always lived in communities, known their neighbours, felt loyalty and affection for the place where they have their home, and Christians more often than not have chosen to worship within their own community. The Church has had a strong sense of mission to that community in which it is set. That world still exists and is worth holding on to. But patterns change and people relate increasingly not through geographical communities but through communities of interest. Modern communication puts them in touch and keeps them in touch in very different ways from the past. The girl walking down the high street doesn't stop and greet her neighbours as she passes them, but she is deep in conversation, with the help of her mobile phone, with someone you cannot see. Her communities are network communities, not geographical ones.

There is, I believe, a need for the Church to be quite counter-cultural about this trend and to draw people, at least sometimes, into communities that transcend networks – celebrating difference, with a variety of age groups, socio-economic groups, interest groups, all gathered under one roof, a microcosm of the kingdom of God. But there is also the need to take these communities of interest seriously and to allow Church to develop within them; that may mean youth congregations, café church, ramblers church, school church and many more. And I do not simply mean offshoots of the conventional parish church, all under the vicar's benevolent eye. I mean groups of Christians, some perhaps with no background in conventional church, who have reached the point in their gatherings that they want to celebrate the sacraments: to initiate through baptism those who have come to faith in that group and to nourish the life of the group through sharing in the Eucharist. In fact that is the moment when a group turns into a church – when it feels the need for sacramental life – and that poses real challenges in terms of church order and ministry. Bishops have a particularly sensitive role in ministering to these communities and holding them within the Church, while resisting the pressure to make them conform in anything except the absolute fundamentals of church life. We have to find paths towards ordained ministry for those who become leaders in emerging churches and we need to be training pioneer ministers who will go and plant churches in some of these network communities. And, if we won't back that, then we are kidding ourselves that we are a mission-shaped Church.

Of course, the more we have cells and networks and fresh expressions and untidiness, the more we need, in all those settings, real understanding of the truth that our baptism makes us members of the one holy catholic and apostolic Church of Jesus Christ, and the more people need to feel a sense of belonging to the universal as much as the local. And the more we need to draw out from among the people of God those whom the Church can ordain as ministers of word and sacrament, who by their presence and their ministry strengthen the relationship between the local and the universal and keep us all together. For in the end we need one holy, catholic, apostolic, untidy, Spirit-filled, mission-shaped Church. Despite its failures, I believe that we have one; we should stop pouring scorn on her, and defend her, believe in her and love her.

5

I believe in the ministry of the baptized

———•◦•———

Entry into the one holy catholic and apostolic Church is by baptism. When people find themselves being called into discipleship by Jesus Christ, they ask for baptism, and it launches them into a life of discipleship and ministry. That, at least, is the theory. It is relatively easy to see this working in a pre-Christian culture, where most people come to faith in adult life, with no previous involvement with the Church. In our western post-Christian culture, it is much more difficult to see. A norm of infant baptism has partially hidden it. A pastoral policy of baptizing infants where the parents have little connection with the local Christian community has obscured it further.

Good work has been done, however, to bring baptism back into the very centre of the life of the Church and to recover as the norm (without ruling out the derivatives like infant baptism) the Christian initiation of adult believers, who then take their place in the Christian community, clearly aware that they belong now to the company of the baptized, committed to being a disciple of Jesus Christ and called to share in the ministry of the Church. There is a long way to go before that recovery is deeply established in the Church, but the process has begun. The difference between older views and the way we might want to express it now is that whereas people used to say, 'I *was* baptized', now they would be encouraged to say, 'I *am* baptized'. Being baptized is a way of life.

So what is baptism all about? It is an extraordinarily rich symbol, many-layered in its meaning. The prayer that the baptizing minister prays over the water at baptism, which reaches its climax in an invocation of the Holy Spirit, exists in a number of versions, but nearly all of them point to this rich tapestry of meaning.

We thank you, almighty God, for the gift of water
to sustain, refresh and cleanse all life.
Over the water the Holy Spirit moved in the beginning of creation.
Through water you led the children of Israel
from slavery in Egypt to freedom in the promised land.
In water your Son Jesus Christ received the baptism of John
and was anointed by the Holy Spirit as the Messiah, the Christ,
to lead us from the death of sin to newness of life.
We thank you, Father, for the water of baptism.
In it we are buried with Christ in his death.
By it we share in his resurrection.
Through it we are reborn by the Holy Spirit . . .
Now sanctify this water that, by the power of your Holy Spirit,
they may be cleansed from sin and born again.

('Prayer over the Water', *Common Worship: Christian Initiation*)

The references to Jesus are in relation to his baptism, his anointing with the Spirit, his death and his resurrection. For the Christian the meaning lies in relation to birth, to cleansing, to refreshment and life, and to death and resurrection. From womb to tomb and beyond, the water of baptism has something to say.

In the 'breaking of the waters' we emerge from the womb into physical life. The water of the font becomes the spiritual equivalent, for it is the place of rebirth. Even Nicodemus, a teacher of Israel, found that difficult to comprehend. He came to Jesus by night, and Jesus himself became the teacher of Nicodemus, helping him to make some sense of being 'born again'. Jesus said to Nicodemus:

'Very truly, I tell you, no one can see the kingdom of God without being born from above.' Nicodemus said to him, 'How can anyone be born after having grown old? Can one enter a second time into the mother's womb and be born?' Jesus answered, 'Very truly, I tell you, no one can enter the kingdom of God without being born of water and Spirit.' (John 3.3–5)

The water of baptism is about rebirth and also about cleansing. This is the aspect of the water that people have held on to at the expense of others – though even then there is some theological confusion as people wrestle with the idea of original sin and the innocence of new-born infants. The sense of wiping the slate clean, of leaving behind the old life and embarking on the new, cleansed and healed, is much easier to appreciate in relation to an adult candidate; in an infant it is the tendency to sin that is part of our human nature, which is therefore present even in a new-born child, that is being washed away.

Important as this is, it is not the primary emphasis of Christian baptism as we receive it from the New Testament. It was indeed the emphasis in John's baptism on the Jordan, which was a baptism of repentance, for the remission of sins. But baptism into Christ has always been understood as something different.

The Christian emphasis is much more on refreshment, life and growth. We wash in water, but we also need to drink water if we are to survive, to live and to grow. The evangelist John has Jesus stand up on the last great day of the Feast of Tabernacles and cry out in the temple:

> 'Let anyone who is thirsty come to me, and let the one who believes in me drink. As the scripture has said, "Out of the believer's heart shall flow rivers of living water."' Now he said this about the Spirit, which believers in him were to receive.   (John 7.37–39)

The fact that Jesus stands and cries out gives his words particular authority. It is a wonderful invitation to find life in him. The source of the water is Jesus, and it is not a drop in the ocean, but flowing rivers of living water. It is an extravagant image signifying vibrant health and life. The water of baptism is entry into the good and abundant life, with constant streams of refreshment. It links, of course, with the vision in Revelation 22 of the 'river of the water of life' with which the Bible ends (v. 1).

But even this very positive image is not the heart of the matter. For the water also spells death – drowning – and new life. It is quite a subtle idea; or, more exactly, it comes to us by a complex route, which takes us back into the early stories of the Old Testament. For the Israelite people the overwhelming experiences of divine activity, of redemption, were in water. It had happened more than once. First there was Noah, who when all the other inhabitants of the world perished was saved with his family and kept safe on board the ark of gopher wood as the waters raged and swelled.

Then there was the Exodus from Egypt led by Moses, the journey that brought them through the Red Sea, in which they would have been drowned (as the pursuing Egyptians were) had it not been for divine intervention, and a later journey across the Jordan into the promised land, the same Jordan in which Jesus was baptized. The experience here was of leaving behind the old life, passing through waters that ought to have been death-dealing but which turned out to be life-giving, and entering into a new future full of promise. The water became the symbol of a kind of death and resurrection.

So, for all that Jesus died on the dry wood of the cross, the tradition speaks of him going 'through the deep waters of death'. For the Christian, the death and resurrection, because they bring salvation, become the new Exodus experience. The New Testament then has only one further step to go. Passing through the waters of baptism, the Christian identifies with Noah and his family, and Moses and his people, but even more with Jesus, in his death and resurrection. Paul urges this understanding on the Christians at Rome when he asks:

> Do you not know that all of us who have been baptized into Christ Jesus were baptized into his death? Therefore we have been buried with him by baptism into death, so that, just as Christ was raised from the dead by the glory of the Father, so we too might walk in newness of life. (Romans 6.3–4)

The emphasis at this point is very much on relationship with Jesus Christ and it is baptism that incorporates new Christians into the Church and gives them new brothers and sisters. But as Paul develops his argument in the letter to the Romans it becomes clear that this dying and rising and this incorporation into Christ has everything to do with the Holy Spirit, the Holy Spirit, 'which believers in [Christ] were to receive'.

> You are not in the flesh; you are in the Spirit, since the Spirit of God dwells in you. Anyone who does not have the Spirit of Christ does not belong to him. But if Christ is in you, though the body is dead because of sin, the Spirit is life because of righteousness. If the Spirit of him who raised Jesus from the dead dwells in you, he who raised Christ from the dead will give life to your mortal bodies also through his Spirit that dwells in you. (Romans 8.9–11)

Because the Spirit blows like the wind and because God is a God of surprises, it is always difficult to tie a particular gift of God to a particular moment, but for the Christian the sense that the Spirit comes to abide in the believer at baptism, never to leave, whatever fresh outpouring there may never be, is important. In baptism the Church celebrates the indwelling of the Spirit. It will be the Spirit who binds the new believer together with the other members of the Church, drawing all together in the fellowship of the baptized. It will be the Spirit who will ensure that the new believer has gifts that can be offered to the Church and used in the building of God's kingdom. In some traditions the giving of the Spirit is identified very clearly with the entry into the water or the pouring of the water – reminiscent of the baptism of Jesus himself, when the Spirit like a dove seemed to hover above him. In other traditions the giving of the Spirit is associated with generous anointing with oil, a rich symbol for a generous gift.

An emphasis on the Holy Spirit as the one who gives gifts and ministries in baptism is explored by Paul more fully in his first letter to the Corinthians. Here he sets out, in one of two passages that have become critical for the development of ministry in the Church in recent years, his picture of how the one Spirit gives a great variety of gifts. The gifts he lists, ones that were clearly evident in the Church at Corinth, concern utterance of wisdom and of knowledge, healing, working of miracles, prophecy, discernment of spirits, speaking in tongues and interpreting such speaking. But there is no suggestion that this list is exhaustive. The gifts of the Spirit are of many different kinds. Paul's whole point in describing them is to show how they all go together to build up the Church, the body of Christ. He has wise things to say about the person, one 'part of the body', who might think their gift to be superior, or indeed inferior, to all the others. Every member of the body has value and all need one another.

The passage, together with one that is similar, though not identical, in Ephesians 4, has come alive for the Church in recent years, partly under the influence of the charismatic movement. It is almost as if its meaning had lain dormant, its full implications lost, for many centuries, but now it speaks with clarity into a new situation and is bringing a fresh approach to Christian ministry.

What is not so often recognized is that Paul specifically relates this talk of the Spirit and the gifts to baptism. In 1 Corinthians 12.13 he says, 'In the one Spirit we were all baptized into one body – Jews or Greeks, slaves or free – and we were all made to drink of the one Spirit.' In Ephesians 4.4–7 he expresses it like this:

There is one body and one Spirit, just as you were called to the one hope of your calling, one Lord, one faith, one baptism, one God and Father of all, who is above all and through all and in all.
But each of us was given grace according to the measure of Christ's gift.

If each of us is given grace according to the measure of Christ's gift, then we can talk of the 'ministry of all the baptized' and of 'every member ministry'. It is a huge shift from the picture of the Church's ministry that seemed to be just about three orders of ministry – bishops, priests and deacons – and everyone else, if they counted at all, was there to support and help the professionals. What has been recovered is a sense that ministry is too important to be left to the professionals and that no person should be denied the opportunity to discern, develop and use their gifts within the ministry of the whole people of God. Put at its most simple, it shifts from a concept of ministry as the work of clergy, helped by laity, to one that sees ministry as the work of the laity, helped by the clergy. That is a major turnaround and is taking time to sink in, but it is true to Scripture and brings new life and energy to the work of ministry.

In one community after another, people are having to work through what this means. It has implications, of course, for the ministry of the ordained. It may change their role – indeed, shifts in our society are changing that role also – but it does not diminish it. Laity who are equipped for ministry, who see themselves as in the front line of God's mission, more than ever have need of what the ordained ministry can provide. Furthermore, there is a deep need for the priest, the holy person, in our culture, modelling a style of life that others would like to discover for themselves. But the important truth is that we see ordained ministers as emerging from the community, from the *laos*, and still being part of it. Their calling needs to be not only a sense of vocation from within themselves but a calling from the community, the pointing of the finger by the local church, challenging people to see what it is God wants them to do.

There will be a greater variety to priesthood. Some members will continue to exercise a ministry, principally pastoral in nature, in particular geographical communities. The 'parish system', though stretched and not sufficient to reach the present generation, still has life and energy in it. Some clergy will minister in chaplaincies, in hospitals, prisons, the forces, schools and workplaces. There will be theologians and teachers. Pioneer ministers will break new ground. Others will be called to oversight ministry, leading teams of lay people and clergy, which requires gifts of strategic leadership. Despite this variety of emphasis, all will need to be collaborators. The day of the solo-minister is all but gone.

Some have feared that two classes of priesthood will emerge, especially between stipendiary and non-stipendiary ministers and between team leaders and pastors. But this should not be the case, for what all priests have in common is far more fundamental than what differs from minister to minister. The ordination rite speaks of them as 'servants and shepherds, messengers, watchmen and stewards' (*Common Worship: Ordination Services*). What is required of them is a disciplined and prayerful holiness, a desire to model a Christ-like life and a passion to communicate the love of God. This they do above all through their particular calling as ministers of word and sacrament. They are ministers of what has formed them and continues to form them, for study of the Scriptures and reverence for the sacraments need to be at the heart of their ministry.

Leadership in the Church is not restricted to ordained ministers, nor is every priest required to exercise leadership – except in a very gentle manner, leading people to Christ. But the requirements of the Church in our own day have put a greater emphasis on qualities of leadership and the Church is in need of these. But leadership is a word and concept that sits uncomfortably with an understanding of ministry as servanthood. Jesus speaks more readily of himself as a servant than as a leader, though he does both. Indeed it is just when he demonstrates his servanthood most tellingly, in the washing of the disciples' feet, that he declares himself in John 13 to be 'Master and Lord'. 'That is what I am,' he says; he does not, in the end, deny his role of leadership, but he demonstrates very powerfully how it is to be exercised. He models 'servant-leadership'. It has almost become a cliché, and that is a pity, for it is something crucial for those who are given authority in the Church.

It makes the ministry of the deacon all the more crucial. Most of those ordained to this ministry are transitional deacons on their way to ordination as a priest – not all, however, for some have discerned that God's calling to them is to be a deacon, and nothing further in terms of ordination, for the rest of their working life. But for those for whom it is part of a journey into priestly ministry, it is like the laying of a firm foundation, a first layer of service and servanthood, a down-on-your-knees ministry with a special concern for the poor, the marginalized and the dispossessed. They model that Christ-like ministry both for the laity and for their fellow clergy. Only when that firm foundation is in place can there be added other layers where leadership features more strongly. Leadership can be laid on top of that solid layer of diaconal ministry, which needs always to give shape to what follows and never be left behind. 'Once a deacon, always a deacon,' clergy say to one another and, if they are wise, they neither forget it nor cease to act in accordance with it.

The ministry of both priest and deacon is related to that of bishop. In the case of priests, they relate to the bishop because he (and she in some countries – one day not too far away, please God, in England too) is the president of the college of presbyters of the diocese; this is why all the members of the college lay their hands on the ordinands at the ordination of priests. In the case of deacons, their relationship is very much that of those who minister *with* the bishop; this is why he alone lays hands upon them at ordination. The bishop is the link between the local and the universal. He moves around the local communities, reminding them that they are part of something bigger than the house church or the parish or the benefice. He tries to fulfil his apostolic ministry as pastor, teacher, leader of mission and principal minister of the sacraments and to be a sign of unity. The episcopal ring I wear on the fourth finger of my right hand has inscribed upon it the Latin words *ut unum sint* ('that they may be one'). It is what Jesus prayed for his disciples and it is the prayer of every bishop as he tries to hold together the different communities that have been entrusted to him, even though day to day he shares that ministry with the priests and deacons – 'this cure which is both yours and mine', as he says when he licenses a priest to a new ministry. It follows that the Church can only function effectively if every church member in the diocese wants to be in communion with their bishop.

This ministry as a sign of unity goes beyond the task of holding together the communities that make up the diocese. The bishop's task is to relate the local church, and the diocese, to the universal

Church. When the bishops come together in a national 'house' or 'college', or better still when they come together in a worldwide fellowship such as the Anglican Communion, the task of each is to represent the local diocese to the rest of the Church. On returning home their task is to represent the wisdom of the universal to the local. That is the bishop's ministry, to move between local and universal, reminding the one of the other, interpreting the one to the other. In this way the smallest, most remote and perhaps hopelessly parochial church is drawn into communion with every other Christian across the world.

There is a slight air of unreality about this. In a divided Church, it is impossible to achieve universal consensus. The most that can be managed is a decision by the part of the universal Church to which one belongs, whether it be the Roman Catholic Church or the Anglican Communion or the Lutheran World Federation or some other grouping; and even here within one of these more limited expressions of the worldwide there can be dreadful tensions and disagreements. Yet the task of the bishop is to try to work creatively and patiently within the constraints and to seek the highest level of episcopal collegiality that is possible, always wanting to be a sign of unity, so that the Church might be one.

The Church consists of men and women and children too (children are never 'the Church of tomorrow'; they are part of the Church of today from the moment of their baptism) and so it should follow that since deacons, priests and bishops are chosen from among the whole people of God some will be male and some will be female. Something is wrong when, in the sanctuary of the local church, all those who minister around the altar, ordained and lay, are of one gender. Something is equally wrong – and it is something deeper even than injustice; it is a false representation of the body of the Christ who is a person of the Trinity beyond gender – when in the councils of the worldwide Church all those who hold the Church together and guard its faith and its fellowship are of one gender. In the Church of today this means that the office of bishop must be opened up to women, who are as able as men to lead and pastor the Church of God, to teach the faith and to reflect the character of God.

Some people see this as a premature development; they plead that the Church should hold back until there can be consensus across the traditions. It is an attractive notion in theory. It would be wonderful if it could be like that. But the truth is that in a divided Church it is the vocation of one part of the Church to innovate, in response to the Spirit's guiding, and thus to model for the rest of the Church a development that later others will embrace. The churches of the Reformation did this in relation to married clergy, and more fundamentally in making the Scriptures and the liturgy available in the language of the people. They did not wait for a universal agreement. They led the way. Sometimes that is where the Spirit leads. And where the Spirit has been at work there is, normally, very soon good fruit to show. In the case of the ordination of women to the priesthood in the Church of England, many years of women's priesthood has produced a wonderful harvest and added a rich complementarity to the ministry of men. Men and women together have been able to mirror more effectively the ministry of Christ and the character of God. The ordination of women to the episcopate will simply make that complete and be another blessing.

Ordination, whether as deacon, priest or bishop, is important in giving to the Church ministers who are themselves God's gift to his people. That's how Paul understands it in Ephesians 4.11–12: 'The gifts he gave were that some would be apostles, some prophets, some evangelists, some pastors and teachers, to equip the saints for the work of ministry, for building up the body of Christ.' But ordination can never compete with baptism, which is the foundation call into discipleship and ministry. Ordination simply builds upon it. The ministry of the Church is a ministry of men and women, lay and ordained, all of them bound together by the one baptism in which Christ claims them for himself and the Holy Spirit plants within them the needful gifts of grace to fulfil their calling.

6

I believe in Christian values

<hr />

The ministry of the whole people of God leads them into real, committed engagement with the society in which they are set. To exercise that ministry they have to be confident about what they need to say to the society of which they are part. In this and the next chapter I address related questions about the kind of values our society needs and what kind of society we want to create. Later I shall write about the tension between the kingdom of God and the Church of Christ, and between idealism and pragmatism in making ethical decisions, and then about four aspects of society – God-fearing society (which will include quite a lot on multiculturalism), global society, just society and inclusive society. You can immediately see how that overlaps with Christian values, which is where I need to begin.

The first question we face in relation to Christian values is this. On what basis do we decide (if decide is the right word) our values? Even that question, as you can see, is not without a problem. Are our values something we decide or are we given them? If we receive them, do they come from God or from the Scriptures or from our culture? For the time being I am going to stick with 'decide', believing our Christian values are things we work at, rather than simply accept as a given.

Many Christians would go first to the Ten Commandments. Some will be used to reading these on the east wall of their church, alongside the Creed and the Lord's Prayer. Some will have grown up on the Ten Commandments, recited week by week in the Prayer Book Communion Service. For some it is a deep regret that you hear and see the Ten Commandments much less often nowadays. There is little agreement about their status for the Christian world.

We need, of course, to see them in their context. They are ten very simple, straightforward rules (more negative than positive) that were given to a group of nomadic tribes living under canvas in a wilderness somewhere between Egypt and the Promised Land. That's where they come from. Those are the conditions for which they were given. With this origin you can see how two very different views can emerge. One view says that human nature does not change at a basic level. What were God-given laws for those nomadic people millennia ago are equally applicable today – they are given to us too. The other view says that a set of simple rules for primitive peoples needs to be superseded by rules of far greater sensitivity, subtlety and complexity if they are to be of any use to the fast-changing and immensely complex society in which we live. Not I think that anybody would want to say that the Ten Commandments have nothing to say to us. But do they get us very far? Do we not need a much more subtle code of behaviour? How far does 'Thou shalt do no murder' get me in relation to, say, justification for war, or euthanasia, assisted suicide or abortion?

We have to ask, given the character and the teaching of Jesus, whether we can adopt as our own a set of commandments that make no mention of love. At this point it is helpful to introduce what Jesus had to say when asked which was the greatest of the commandments, in Mark 12. He did not repeat the Ten. He came out with something different, itself almost a direct quotation from Deuteronomy, but rather different in character from the Ten: '"You shall love the Lord your God with all your heart, and with all your soul, and with all your mind, and with all your strength." The second is this, "You shall love your neighbour as yourself"' (Mark 12.30–31).

People have sometimes labelled this the 'Summary of the Law'; but, of course, the moment you call it that you have labelled it in such a way that you have narrowed its meaning. Is Jesus giving a summary, a kind of shorthand version, of the Ten Commandments, or is he saying something new and radical? My own view is that it is the latter. He is giving a new commandment – love God and love your neighbour as yourself. It is new because it is about love. It is new because it is all positive – it is what you must do rather than what you must not do. It is new because it is actually much more demanding. It does not give a quick checklist; it is sufficiently all-embracing that there is no area of human behaviour where it does not need to be applied. And it is new because it makes you think; it makes ethics something you have to struggle with. There are no simple rules on a plate; you have to take each and every moral situation and work at how loving God and loving neighbour and indeed loving self helps to shape appropriate behaviour. Those Ten Commandments are there in the background and only a fool would write them off, but we have been given a new commandment – at one level more flexible, at another more all-embracing, more demanding.

If that has been true through 2,000 years of Christian history, it has never been more so than today. We live in a postmodern society where there are few enough common values, and a complexity of moral issues. I sometimes (though not often) envy those who fail to see the complexity, the people for whom the issues are straightforward. For them right and wrong are very black and white. The teaching of the Bible is clear and unequivocal. Sin is easily identifiable and a call for repentance the only remedy. But in the end it is those people who find it all uncomplicated whom I find most difficult. I can cope with those who come to different conclusions from me about moral issues, providing they can see the complexity. Let me try to explain what I mean.

Why are things complex? There are three answers, all related to the Scriptures. The first is that the Scriptures themselves are not usually internally consistent. Different biblical writers say different things. The New Testament, the Christian Scriptures, often takes a different line from the Old Testament, the Hebrew Scriptures, which is hardly surprising when the Bible tells the story of a pilgrimage of religious understanding over more than a thousand years. And even when specific verses of Scripture seem to point in one direction, the overall thrust of Scripture may seem to be in a very different one.

To take one example, the specific words of Paul in his letters seem to recognize slavery as a natural part of the social order (see Colossians 3), yet the overall message of the New Testament, and indeed of Paul himself, would lead one to believe that slavery was an offence against human dignity and freedom. The particular is at odds with the overall message. There is internal inconsistency in the Scriptures if you set verse against verse, though that is hardly ever a helpful thing to do.

Second, Scripture does not engage with modern medical and psychological knowledge. Indeed it does not – it cannot – engage with much post-Enlightenment knowledge. Its writers, inspired as they were, lived in a different world. There are key issues on which the Bible has nothing specific to say, for instance in relation to genetic engineering or in vitro fertilization.

Third, there is another inconsistency, not this time in the Bible itself but in the way we use it. We pick and choose (and we do not all pick and choose the same things, which is why we fall out) which parts of Scripture to see as binding commandment and which to see as unattainable ideal. So a Christian may be very intolerant of homosexual practice, seeing it as clearly contrary to the teaching of Paul, as in Romans 1, for example (Jesus never mentions the issue), but at the same time quite relaxed about divorce and remarriage, on which Jesus has some fairly harsh things to say in Mark 10. We use Scripture inconsistently.

So what is the way through in all this complexity so that we can lead ethical lives and be in a position to give moral guidance to others?

We need first to establish the ideals that Jesus seems to urge upon us and that seem to receive general support in Scripture, certainly in the New Testament. Of course, even this involves debate, but we do not start from scratch, so to speak, and we are not debating in a vacuum, because the Church has come to a common mind on many issues and this body of teaching is there in place.

Let me give you a couple of examples of these ideals. 'God's intention is that sexual union should find its expression in marriage.' Or, 'Human life is sacred: human beings have no right to destroy it.' Those are ideals. We need not only to establish them but to keep on urging them. There is no point in having hidden ideals. We need to proclaim them loud and clear. But at the same time we should recognize that in a fallen world these ideals are not always attainable by everyone. We all, in some areas, fail to attain the ideal. We get caught up in situations, especially when it comes to our relationships, where we try to live with integrity in a situation that we know falls short of the ideal. We need to be helped to live creatively within that situation – we may feel trapped, aware of our frailty, possibly recognizing our sin, but knowing ourselves to be doing our best.

Consider this story. John falls in love with Clare. Clare was first married, too young, while she was a student, and it ended quite quickly in divorce. It left her with her self-esteem in tatters. In the way people do, she married again on the rebound, and this marriage produced two children. But then there was domestic violence, she ended up in a women's refuge, her children went into care for a while, and, of course, there was another divorce. Some time after that John came along; he really loved this very battered, broken Clare and he was immensely kind to her children. She began to blossom again in the embrace of this good man who loved her and treated her well. He wanted to marry her, but after her previous experiences she could not bring herself to enter marriage again. And yet she needed him and he was the instrument of her healing. They are a family unit now, and the kids are secure.

What is their moral position? They are, as we say, 'living in sin'. Those for whom these decisions are easy, those with the moral certainties, will say that here is a situation to condemn. For myself, I do not want to say that 'anything goes'; I intend to go on gently urging the Christian ideal of marriage. I do not want to say that there is no human failure or sin in that situation, but I see that there is a lot of goodness and it seems that what is going on in that relationship is a bit of resurrection.

What I believe the Church has nearly always done in relation to moral issues (not just sexual ones, but they are the ones we seem as a Church to be obsessed with now) is to take three or four insights and build from them some principles and then exercise pastoral care. The insights are these. First, the teaching of the Scriptures. As I have already said, that in itself involves a certain amount of complexity, but the Scriptures are to be taken with the utmost seriousness and we need to get hold of what they are really saying. Second, we put alongside it what we call 'tradition' – and that simply means 2,000 years of patient reflection of what Scripture means, often in the light of changing culture. The tradition is the cumulative wisdom of our Christian forebears on the subject and that too needs to be taken with great seriousness.

The third insight is 'reason'. We bring to bear our intellectual and critical faculties on an ethical issue. And that is the point when we may have to feed in new knowledge, very often from the sciences. Although the last word has not been said, there is a vast amount of knowledge available to us, for instance about the nature of homosexuality, that our forebears simply could not know. It would be extraordinary if we dismissed that knowledge as irrelevant in trying to establish a contemporary Christian ethic.

Scripture, tradition and reason has been the classic approach to Christian belief – theological and ethical – and one particularly adopted in Anglicanism. But I said three or four insights; I am conscious that people sometimes want to add a fourth one: experience. What is there that I can see, or hear, or experience for myself in any other way, that also needs to be taken into account? If I observe that the love between John and Clare, even though it is outside marriage, is a setting in which healing is happening for a whole family (and God is the giver of healing), does what I observe make a difference as I try to reach an ethical view? That is bringing experience to bear.

We have to bring together these four insights and then exercise some pastoral sensitivity and care; this may involve helping people to recognize sin, but it may also involve seeing signs of grace in them.

I am, of course, worried by my own line of argument, for I do not want to say that the language of sin is outmoded. It is not outmoded. It remains crucial for our understanding of our own relationship with God and the relationship of humankind with its Creator. The sin in any situation needs to be recognized. The woman taken in adultery in John's Gospel is not condemned by Jesus. He is not into condemnation, except perhaps of scribes and Pharisees. But nor does he condone. He says to the woman, 'Has no one condemned you? . . . Neither do I condemn you. Go your way, and from now on do not sin again' (John 8.10–11). Christ recognizes the sin. He does not deny it. He does not condemn. But he does challenge – he issues an invitation to a better way. So we go on having a duty of identifying the sin (especially in ourselves). Christian ethics never degenerates into 'anything goes'.

But I continue to be concerned that, in failing to engage with the complexities, and in just repeating the rules, we miss opportunities and indeed fail the world around us. My worry is that because of our blanket condemnations we do not make distinctions. Are John and Clare – living faithfully together, with no other sexual partners, caring for children, experiencing the grace of healing – morally in the same place as the man who, besides having a wife, keeps a mistress and occasionally visits a brothel? Surely not, but the Church is simply heard to say that sex outside marriage is sinful, as if the two cases were the same.

What about the two men who fell in love with one another 20 years ago, set up house together and have now entered a civil partnership? Are they morally in the same place as the promiscuous young man, or woman, who has a different sexual partner every time they go to a party? As long as the Church cannot find the courage to face these questions, we have nothing to say to our society as it struggles with right and wrong. We make our stand in a place so far removed from where most people are that they cannot believe we have anything to say that might help them find the values to shape their lives. We are so unreal as to be irrelevant. And it goes further than that. For the 'they' for whom we have nothing to say is often the same set of people as ourselves. It isn't somebody else's daughter who lives with her boyfriend – it will be true of people reading this. It isn't somebody else who is gay – it will be true of people reading this. Or if it is not, it is because the Church is failing to be the welcoming, embracing body of the broken Christ.

I suppose I have fallen for our current fashionable over-obsession with sexual ethics. But I think that the principles apply much more broadly. We need to establish the ideals, and we need to keep urging them. But then we have to recognize that in a fallen world people cannot always live up to them. We bring the insights of Scripture, tradition, reason and experience to bear. And then we speak and act pastorally. We look for repentance, but look too for signs of grace.

I would like to change tack now and look at Christian values from a different angle. I want to plead that we find our Christian values by looking at Jesus. Even more than looking to the commandments, even more than taking together the insights of Bible, tradition, reason and experience, we find our Christian values by looking at Jesus. Christian values are Christ-like values.

Jesus gave priority to love. He directed his love, and told us to direct our love, towards God, neighbour, enemy and self. Love for God came first. To have God in the picture shapes our ethical response in all sorts of situations, for it seeks to bring our behaviour into line with God's purpose for his creation and his sovereignty over all things.

Jesus then puts love for neighbour second only to love for God. He makes it clear that 'neighbour' should be understood very broadly; it includes the people you least expect, it includes the people you rather despise. Your neighbour could be anyone. In another setting, he produces yet another category of person to love, the enemy. He certainly modelled that for us, as he met with opposition and faced his Passion.

But then there is the element of loving we sometimes fail to recognize. He tells us to love ourselves. 'Love your neighbour as yourself' (Matthew 22.39). There is, of course, a wrong sort of self-love, one that is self-deceiving and an obstacle to a loving relationship with others. Nevertheless, when we do not see ourselves as God sees us, as a precious and deeply loved child of God, when we lack self-esteem, we lack the Christ-like value we need to give ourselves if we are to flourish and to have love to give to others.

At the heart of Christ-like values are these four elements of loving – love God, love neighbour, love enemy, love self. In Jesus we see that loving pressed as far as it can go; it was for love for God and for the whole human race, for neighbour writ large and enemy too, that he went to his Passion and was lifted up on the cross. Christ-like values embrace sacrifice and sometimes suffering too. And one might almost stop there. In a sense Jesus did stop there, when he said that 'on these two commandments hang all the law and the prophets' (Matthew 22.40).

But we are wise to press on a little further. When we look at Jesus, we see other values that might shape our behaviour. I want to add four things to Christ-like sacrificial loving.

The first is that Jesus built community. One of his values was to draw people together, to give them a shared experience. Even though there were moments when he needed to be alone, there was little rest from the labour of drawing people into relationship, whether it was a great crowd to be taught and fed in the desert, or that base company of friends that he turned into a community of apostles, or that trusted little circle of intimates, Peter, James and John, who were allowed to draw close on the mountain of transfiguration and in the garden of Gethsemane. And, of course, whatever we have made of her, there is the Church. He gave us the Church. Jesus built community. Christ-like values take that very seriously.

Second, Jesus was self-effacing, self-denying even, and he invited his disciples to deny themselves also and take up their cross to follow him. I don't think that this contradicts loving oneself, though it is a bit of a paradox. Loving yourself is knowing your value in God's sight, guarding your self-esteem, giving time and space to what affirms your humanity, your selfhood. But to be self-effacing is to embrace humility, as Jesus did, to be content to see yourself least in the kingdom of heaven (but in the kingdom of heaven and so loved by God); to be self-denying is to be disciplined and to willingly walk a road of sacrifice. To be Christ-like is to be both self-effacing and self-denying.

Third, one of the key messages of John's Gospel is Jesus' statement: 'I came that they may have life, and have it abundantly' (John 10.10) – 'in all its fullness', as another version translates it. Jesus was, and is, life-affirming. There is place for denial, of course, but he is never life-denying. He is death-defying, because he is life-affirming. That is all acted out on the big stage of the empty tomb and the resurrection, but all the way Jesus raises people up, gives them life, affirms, restores. A Christian lifestyle is one that consistently values life and wants to improve the quality of life for all around.

Christian values include building community, denying self and affirming life. But there is yet one more fundamental value for the Christian. It is generosity. It has to be, doesn't it, if we are made in the image of a generous God, who alongside everything else gave us his Son and in his Son his very self? Paul, in 2 Corinthians 8, speaks of the generosity of Jesus Christ, who though he was rich, for our sake became poor, so that we might become rich. Generosity is the mark of the gracious God; generosity made Jesus our courteous, forgiving, healing Saviour; generosity is a deeply Christ-like Christian value.

What, then, are the values that I learn from Jesus Christ, by which I want to lead my life and which I want to commend to my society? They are the value of love (for God, for neighbour, for enemy and for self), the value of community, the value of self-denial, the value of life itself, the value of generosity.

How does that play into our twenty-first-century secular culture? At certain points it speaks the same language as people of other faiths, those of non-religious ideologies or philosophies and those of thoughtfulness who struggle to create their own moral code. That is why we can join hands with people who speak of common values and spiritual values. We are told that there is a great hunger in our society for both of these – common values that we seem to have lost and spiritual values that rescue us from materialism – but that people are not turning to the Church for help in finding them. That is greatly to our shame, and we have to plead guilty to a deafening silence when we could have been part of a real debate. But I know that we have a distinctive contribution to make. That contribution brings in the religious dimension – loving God – and the Christ dimension, for though Jesus is much more than this, he is, among other things, an exemplar of the moral life for those who will model their values on him.

7

I believe in a new society

—◆·◆·◆—

'I believe in an amazing God' is a different sort of statement from
'I believe in a new society'. The first is a statement of what I believe
to be true, the second is an aspiration. I want there to be a new
society – God-fearing, global, just, inclusive, moral – but we are
a long way from it and so to say that I believe in it is to say that
I commit myself to work for it, to turn vision into reality. I do
that even though I know that this will always be an imperfect
world. Not every ideal will be realized. But that does not remove
the obligation to try to make the dreams come true.

Too many Christians live in the unreal world of the Church.
The Church can be beastly, but on the whole it is a rather reassuring
and comforting world to live in. We can be so preoccupied with
living in it, or even reforming it, that we cease to live in the world.
But that is where God wants us to be. It is the world he wants us
to change. John does not tell us that God so loved the Church
that he sent his Son, but that God so loved the world. John,
remember, also tells us that Jesus came that everyone might have
life, have it 'more abundantly', in all its fullness. Belonging to the
Church commits us to wanting to change the world for the better;
it commits us to the creation of a new society of justice, peace
and love.

To put it differently, the mission of God is not fundamentally
to grow the Church, but to grow the kingdom of heaven on earth.
'Kingdom' is an important word in the thinking and teaching of
Jesus. It is a slightly difficult word to get hold of today, when neither
kings nor kingdoms are what they used to be. But we say happily
enough – it trips off the tongue – 'Your kingdom come, your will be
done, on earth as it is in heaven' in the Lord's Prayer and we need
to see how that commits us to a new world order. The kingdom of
God, as we picture it in heaven, is a communion of justice, peace and

love. The task is to strive to establish that on earth, not just in the Church (though that is a challenge) but in our wider society.

I want to say some fairly idealistic things about the way the world needs to be and you might think me hopelessly naive. So, before the idealism and the vision, let's acknowledge a problem. The problem is this. Every time we appear to make progress, sometimes phenomenal progress, in creating a better world, so that some great evil seems to have been banished from the earth, we discover that either some new evil has taken its place or that our original victory was more hollow than we thought. In 2007 we celebrated the 200th anniversary of the Act to abolish the slave trade. What a huge step forward for humankind! But then, 200 years later, we learn about the sex industry and child pornography in the Far East, and nearer home the exploitation of illegal immigrants, and we wonder how much slavery there is still in our world. Or we rejoice in the proud claim that after 1945 we have had comparative peace in Europe, but then we learn about Bosnia, not so very far away, with war and ethnic cleansing of a sort we believed we had banished from our continent, if not from the face of the earth. We celebrate that we have beaten polio and reduced TB, but then comes the scourge of HIV & AIDS. How much nearer is the new society that we yearn for?

One of my favourite hymns, at Christmas and at Michaelmas, is Edmund Sears' carol, 'It came upon the midnight clear'. It is full of nineteenth-century optimism.

> For lo! The days are hastening on,
> By prophet bards foretold,
> When, with the ever-circling years,
> Comes round the age of gold;
> When peace shall over all the earth
> Its ancient splendours fling,
> And the whole world give back the song
> Which now the angels sing.
> 'It came upon the midnight clear', *New English Hymnal*

I love to sing it, but I don't quite believe it. The age of gold is not just round the corner. The Christian is realistic about the human condition. We live in a fallen world; even the creation is infected. There will always be war, there will always be injustice, there will always be wickedness. Evil is constantly at work. But the calling of the Christian, working with any person who seeks the common good, is to be on the side of the angels, to be persevering for the values of the kingdom of heaven on the earth. We need to place ourselves firmly alongside the Lord in his mission to bring life in all its fullness and not to be disheartened by the fact that we shall have limited success. We live in an age when the majority feels powerless to make a difference for the better. We need to be people who don't give up like that, whatever the cost.

We continue to need prophets, deeply uncomfortable individuals who take things to their logical conclusions when sane people see that it's impossible, or who spell out the overwhelming message of the Scriptures when the rest of us have seen the need to compromise. Let me give an example. There was a very single-minded priest called Sidney Hinkes who died in 2006. Sidney devoted much of his life to the cause of Christian pacifism. He was a key member of what some might regard as a no-hope society, the Anglican Pacifist Fellowship. He wrote about pacifism and protested about wars; no evidence you could produce about the need to stand up to evil forces, militarily if necessary, made any impression on Sidney. He was firm in his convictions, not least because if you take the plain meaning of Scripture and what Jesus says about turning the other cheek, pacifism is right. Certainly in the early centuries Christians thought that their faith was incompatible with military service. In my view Sidney Hinkes was wrong. There are some circumstances in this fallen world where the teaching of Jesus is impossible idealism and the Christian is right to take up arms. But I am profoundly thankful that Sidney Hinkes existed and held obstinately on to views that to me looked less and less defensible. We need the prophets, who will not compromise, to hold before us the vision of the kingdom of justice, peace and love, when we are in danger of losing sight of it. The rest of us may have to compromise. In the area of ethics we compromise all the time. But we should honour the prophet, especially the one who keeps some unpalatable Scriptures before us. We should defend the protester, even when we believe he or she is wrong. We should have a bias for the non-conformist. All of them have an important role in challenging us lest we get sucked into the establishment or too easily adopt the attitudes of the culture in which we live.

With that in the background, I'd like to look at the society for which we are working under these headings: God-fearing society, global society, just society and inclusive society. I also believe we need a moral society and I tried to engage with that in the previous chapter.

First, God-fearing society. That sounds, I concede, like a profoundly unfashionable suggestion. For what we have urged upon us today is either a multicultural society or a secular society. We live, certainly, in a pluriform society. Even within one nation, we clearly do not share nearly as much in common in terms of our philosophy and our values as used to be the case. As Christians we probably cannot help regretting the passing of an age when the Church and the Christian faith seemed to be a very strong influence in our society, though that influence could make us fairly complacent. The more competitive arena in which we operate now can make our contribution sharper.

But what about multicultural society? The Christian Church needs to engage with other religions, and especially with Islam, for the world's sake. We do not need to deny the uniqueness of our faith – our claims for Jesus as much more than a prophet, as the only begotten Son of God – in order to talk graciously, honestly and, yes, lovingly with our brothers and sisters of one of the other great Abrahamic religions. At the very least we owe them the courtesy of being sufficiently interested in them as human beings and fellow citizens to want to know about their faith and the shape it gives to their lives. Beyond that I hope we will sometimes want to be in dialogue with them, to ponder with them on the mystery of life, the nature of God, the problem of evil, the hope of heaven.

And as part of that we should grasp the opportunity to say with gentle conviction who Jesus is for us. If we see too much risk in saying prayers with them, at least we ought, I believe, to be ready to sit in prayerful silence with them, with people who certainly take their prayer life a good deal more seriously than many Christians. I believe that there is a further stage to which we should be prepared to go, and that is to stand alongside them on a number of ethical and social issues and speak for the people of faith into a secular culture that has lost touch with God and his laws.

Religions are not all the same. It is only people of no religion who seem to believe that to be the case. Christianity and Islam are very different. But it does not follow that we cannot sometimes talk with one another and speak together to our society. We can and we must.

Multiculturalism has been pursued fairly relentlessly for a generation and it has been regarded as politically incorrect to challenge it. But there has been some new thinking of late about it and I believe it is right to be looking afresh at this area of our national life in a search for a balance between encouraging diversity on the one hand and furthering integration into one society on the other. But I hope the pendulum will not swing back too far. I do believe that our society has been delightfully enriched by people who have settled here and shared their values and their customs. I say values as well as customs, for though the customs may be appealing – festivals and carnivals and exotic dress and rich food – it is the values, the morality and spirituality, and the community instincts that have probably enriched us the more. A return to a white Anglo-Saxon monoculture, even if it were possible, would be a grave impoverishment. I think that multicultural Britain looks just a little more like the kingdom of God.

But the current thinking is that multiculturalism has not delivered integration. Minority communities have been so encouraged to keep their ethnic identity that they have not been integrated into Britain. Clearly it is true that this integration has not taken place as much as it ought, though I suspect the reasons for this are quite complex. A ghetto community is created more by poverty and where cheaper housing is to be found than by a desire to stand apart from the majority culture. There is a case for some fresh initiatives, especially in the education system, to help ethnic minorities feel more at home with the predominant British culture, even as that culture itself changes and develops. There is a need for fresh thinking about a patriotism appropriate to the twenty-first century. Some of this needs to be worked through before we can confidently urge British values on first- and second-generation citizens. What are the British values we want to inculcate as part of the very desirable process of integration?

One of them, I believe, is a reverence for the Christian tradition that has shaped our nation's life, even though we have too often fallen short of its ideals. Our laws and our customs, our history and our heritage spring from Christian origins. In this area I think we can justly claim that multiculturalism has let us down. For I do not believe that it is just Christian paranoia that is convinced that in the last generation a multicultural, multifaith approach has celebrated

almost everything except Christian culture and Christian faith. There
has been all the nonsense about calling 25 December anything but
Christmas – Winterval, Yuletide, Noel, anything but the Christian
name for a Christian feast. Nobody, I think, has tried to give any
Muslim or Hindu festival a religion-neutral name! Then there has
been an extraordinary reluctance in government (now being over-
come) to believe that heritage and culture are anything to do with
religion or the Church; the Church is denied a place in regional
cultural consortia as if its role were quite irrelevant, when the reality is that the Church cares for the majority of the great heritage
buildings of the land, and churches and church halls play host to
more cultural events than any other buildings. The Church sometimes
seems to be airbrushed out of the nation's picture of its common
life, when the truth is that it is there in every community and, for
all the assaults of secularism, there remains a deep Christian influence
in almost every aspect of our national life.

What we need to work for, and even stand up for and demand, is
a level playing field, where the Christian story can be freely told, the
Christian festivals celebrated, the Christian heritage recognized, the
Christian contribution to our life honoured and valued. It is not
Muslims who want to stop that, but a kind of secularism, fuelled by
a hostile national media, that wants to push all religion, especially
the Christian religion, to the margins. A truly multifaith, multicultural Britain will not allow that to happen. Multifaith multiculture
includes Christian faith and Christian culture.

Other religions respect this and indeed rely on us to be the lead
player in making this a God-fearing society, rather than a godless
secular culture. Whether, long term, the Christian Church should
have its unique place in relation to the British constitution and establishment is a difficult question. Some things that work surprisingly
well, like the way we appoint our senior clergy that involves both the
Crown and the Prime Minister's office, are difficult to justify. The
presence of bishops in the House of Lords will not go unchallenged
at the next round of revision. The coronation oath and indeed the
setting of the coronation within an Anglican Eucharist have their
problems in twenty-first-century Britain. The nature of the Church's
relationship with the state will change, probably more by evolution
than revolution, but that need not mean that the contribution of the
Church to society, or the willingness of the nation to hear what the

Church has to say, need disappear. Yes, a society with a place for religious belief and religious values is important.

I believe in a global society. It is principally modern communications that have made us aware that we are citizens of one world. A remote tribe in a primitive society has little sense of a world beyond its community, certainly no loyalty to it. For much of human history, the largest loyalty that people have had is for their nation or their country, right or wrong. And look at the waste of human life that that has produced in Europe over the centuries. But modern communications enable us to see a whole world and to be in touch with every part of the globe, sharing the joys and the sufferings of many different lands and cultures. People have talked of the 'global village'. The Archbishop of York is among those who tell us that we should no longer think or speak of different races, but celebrate only one race, the human race.

Of course, the Church should find this emphasis on the global natural and welcome. After all, we delight to be part of the holy catholic Church and that simply means 'universal'. Global world – universal Church. They are talking our language. And ever since Paul put such emphasis on the fact that there are no divisions between Jew and Gentile, slave and free, male and female, in Christ (Galatians 3.28), we have been committed to one human race and the promise of salvation for the whole world. If God is the universal father, he is the father of one family and all the people of earth are my brothers and sisters.

The truth is that we can have ties of loyalty, of family, at a number of levels. The mistake is to opt for one only, whether it be the very local – caring nothing for the world outside and developing a view of other nations that is protectionist or even racist – or the global, so committed to the welfare of the planet or the relief of famine in Africa that we do not notice the poverty in our own communities. Each of us needs to take seriously these levels of community that all rightly have some call upon our loyalty. And every church needs to ensure that its life and action are committed to these different levels. Again, we need the prophets who will discomfort us lest we lose sight of the total picture. The woman who urges us to support the street children of Bangalore when we think that our priority is the church roof; the man who reminds us that while the children's hospice may be an attractive, popular charity that receives lots of support, the new drugs initiative in our nearest city is receiving less support and maybe that is where we should be putting our money and perhaps our volunteer time as well. And our children who keep challenging us to use our cars less, shower instead of bath, turn off lights – not to save money, but to save the planet, and the fight against global warming starts in actions like that. Yes, we need levels of loyalty, from the very local to the vastly global: one race, one humankind, one world, because there is one God. And for the future of God's world, we either work for its future together or we go down together in a catastrophe of human devising.

A God-fearing society, a global society, a just society. I almost used the word *compassionate* instead of just, and I do think that there is evidence, despite the wickedness and greed in the world, that people care more than they did for those in distress. I think it is partly because we can so cushion ourselves from suffering in the affluent western world that we are more scandalized when we see it in people who have no such cushion. Poverty, starvation and homelessness look even less tolerable when they are totally outside your experience. So we probably are a more compassionate people, and praise the Lord for that. But I chose rather to say that I believe in a *just* society, for I think we miss the point if compassion is our only motive.

The Scriptures do reveal to us a compassionate God, but much more they portray a God who cares for justice and who sometimes, in the pursuit of it, is strong in his judgement on those who practise injustice – see Amos 5 and Micah 6, for example. The prophets of old saw injustice as a particularly dreadful form of godlessness. God is ultimate righteousness and his desire, which he wants us to share, is for everyone to enjoy this world of peace and plenty that he created. The lack of this justice scandalizes God. Compassion is not enough, at least not as our motive. Our motive must be justice.

And that, of course, may lead us into difficult political areas. What does God's justice mean in the Israeli–Palestinian conflict? What does it mean in relation to the invasion of Iraq, with the American President of the time claiming that God sent him in to topple Saddam Hussein, and the then British Prime Minister recognizing, rightly we Christians would believe, that he will have to answer on that issue before the judgement seat of God?

It means, first of all, that we should have absolutely no time for those foolish people who say that you should keep religion out of politics or politics out of religion. They have not begun to understand the nature of God. God cares about justice. Politics is about justice. Christians must care about justice and about politics. If the Church is to be criticized, it should be for remaining silent on some of the political issues of our day, not for speaking out. That is not to say that there will always be one clear and undisputed Christian viewpoint. There are issues on which there can be a unanimous Christian voice that challenges or defends the action of governments, but it is not usually as clear-cut as that. Much more often it is simply a matter of being engaged in the debate, looking for wisdom from Christian Scripture, tradition or experience to find a way through a complex political dilemma. When there is no Christian voice speaking for justice, we have let the God of justice down.

But this also means that the Church needs to have its clearest theological minds at work to help nations make the right decisions. In all the ethical complexities of medical research today, for instance, we need people who bring theological insights to bear. In relation to the future of the planet, the care of the environment, the conservation and sharing of the world's resources, we need those who have reflected deeply and passionately on peace and justice and the integrity of creation. When it comes to decisions on invading sovereign states, removing tyrants or fighting global terror, we need theological minds that can help society to see how the traditional just-war arguments can be interpreted afresh in the changed conditions of international terrorism. In other words, the Church and individual Christians need both to have passion and to be informed.

A God-fearing society, a global society, a just society, an inclusive society. You might accuse me of political correctness, for 'inclusion' is a very fashionable word. If you want some government funding, make sure you are working for social inclusion! But isn't that what the Church, by its very nature, has been trying to do for 2,000 years? Isn't the New Testament an extraordinarily inclusive series of documents? Wasn't Jesus extraordinarily inclusive in the company he kept – men and women, Jews and Gentiles, leprosy sufferers, tax collectors, prostitutes, rich young men and blind beggars? What an inclusive company! And Paul articulates it in Galatians 3.28. Speaking of the Church he says: 'There is no longer Jew or Greek, there is no longer slave or free, there is no longer male and female; for all of you are one in Christ Jesus.'

He is talking of the Church, and if ever the Church were intended to model something for wider society, surely it is this inclusiveness? Of course we have a mixed record. In some ways the Church has always been wonderfully inclusive. No one with faith is forbidden baptism. On the other hand, people with the wrong kind of accent, or even the wrong kind of clothes, let alone the wrong colour of skin, have sometimes been made to feel quite uncomfortable in particular church communities. And it is ironic, and indeed a disgrace, that a Church whose foundation document says that there is no longer male and female is having to learn from the secular world some hard lessons about gender inclusivity.

So, although inclusive society sounds straightforward enough – a natural extension of a theology of one race of humankind, one family of brothers and sisters under the fatherhood of God – it turns out to be another of those rather difficult aspirations. But an important one for the Church to champion.

So, yes, I believe in the creation of a God-fearing, global, just and inclusive society. Furthermore I will work for it, but I won't expect it tomorrow. I know that this world will go on being imperfect, and I am thankful that there will be another one. But that is to talk of heaven.

8

I believe in heaven on earth

———•◆•———

The author of the Revelation to John sees a vision of 'a new heaven and a new earth' that God will create one day. Even more familiar are the words of Jesus within what we have come to call the Lord's Prayer. 'Your kingdom come . . . on earth as it is in heaven,' he has us pray. This chapter explores the life of heaven, but also looks for the establishing of that kingdom of heaven on the earth.

To write or speak of heaven means that we have to use the language of picture and metaphor. We cannot know what heaven is like. We have to acknowledge that what we are trying to describe we can only know by faith and that the words we use are inadequate. Heaven is not, in any usual sense, a 'place'. Yet we find ourselves having to speak as if it were. Heaven will not literally be a feast, as we understand eating and drinking. God will not be seen sitting on a throne. All we can do is paint pictures of something unbelievably wonderful, satisfying and delightful and then know that we have not told the half of it. But it is not a make-believe heaven we have invented to comfort ourselves and protect us from an unpalatable fact that this life might be all there is and eternity a nonsense. The pictures we paint, for all that they cannot be more than that, are out-workings of what Scripture, tradition and reason teach us about the purposes of God. Jesus himself was never in doubt of his return to the Father, nor was he in doubt that there was a room for each one of us in that house of 'many mansions' – see John 14. The overwhelming message of the Scriptures is of a God who has an eternal destiny for us. A Christian faith with no hope in a life to come is simply not Christian faith, as Paul was keen to emphasize in, for example, 1 Corinthians 15.

But if we are to begin exploring heaven, then once again we must explore the nature of God. For however we describe or understand heaven, one thing is constant. At its heart is God. And for Christians the God who is at the heart of heaven is Trinity. God is a relational God, which enables love to be at the heart of heaven also.

For me it is extraordinary that people have made the Trinity difficult. At a certain level it is complex, of course; there are theological issues that scholars engage with in trying to give some definition to the nature of God. The Athanasian Creed is evidence of that and we should not be slipshod in our theological reflection. But there are simple and lovely things to say about the Trinity and these are what people need to hear. There are five truths of the Trinity that continue to enthral me.

The first is this. The Trinity is a mystery. But it is not the kind of mystery you need to solve. It is not one you have to explain. It is a mystery you are invited to enter and to enjoy. If you have never allowed yourself to dwell in this mystery before (though you probably have without knowing it), then when you do so you will find it is like entering a new relationship. There is joy, surprise, a bit of puzzlement ('what's happening to me here?'), there is a sense of being drawn deeper, there is energy, there is love. If you have experienced it, you will know that entering the mystery of the Trinity is like committing yourself to a friend or a lover; and you will also know that if you neglect that relationship or take it for granted you will lose the joy of the relationship. But come back to it with your eyes open wider and there is new potential for joy, for surprise, for puzzlement ('what's happening to me now?') and, wonderfully, you find yourself drawn deeper still. That's the way I believe it can be for you and me with God, who is Trinity. The Trinity is a mystery into which we can enter.

The second thing is that although we cannot in this life penetrate to the heart of the mystery, that does not matter; we don't need to. We simply have to allow ourselves to be drawn in a little way and we immediately meet overwhelming love. And love is not all that we meet. We see unutterable beauty. We encounter unimaginable holiness. We witness unexpected intimacy. We are touched by transforming grace. But what we meet first and experience most deeply, if only we can open ourselves – body, mind and spirit, our entire being with its longings – is love.

For what the Trinity is about is the Father loving the Son, the Son loving the Father, the Spirit the love that flows between them. It is the life, the love, that was there before the world was made. It is the life, the love, that was there before Jesus walked the earth: the Father loving the Son, the Son loving the Father, the Spirit the love that flows between them.

W. H. Vanstone expressed this in *Love's Endeavour, Love's Expense*:

> In the dynamic relationship within the being of the Trinity, love is already present, already active, already completed and already triumphant: for the love of the Father meets with the perfect response of the Son. Each, one might say, endlessly enriches the other: and this rich and dynamic interrelationship is the being and life of the Spirit.
>
> W. H. Vanstone, *Love's Endeavour, Love's Expense*

It is the love that caused the Father to send the Son. It is the love that came down at Christmas. It is the love that took Jesus to the cross. It is the love that burst the tomb open. It is the love that was poured out on Mary at the annunciation, on Jesus at his baptism, on the Church on the day of Pentecost. It is the love that enfolds us from birth to death and beyond. But it has its existence, its reality, in the being of the Trinity.

Third, this creative love is never used up, never drained dry; it is always recreating, always refreshing, and – this is the crucial truth – always overflowing. Within the Trinity there is more love than is needed, more than can be contained. It overflows and runs all over the earth and it enters every human heart that is ready to receive it, taking away the heart of stone. Flowing from the Godhead, from the loving of the Father and the Son and the Holy Spirit, is enough love, and more than enough, to sustain the world God first created out of love and then redeemed by love.

The fourth thing is that we do not have to draw very near this mystery of the Trinity before we find ourselves being beckoned in to its life, its love. That wonderful icon by Rublev referred to earlier showing the 'hospitality of Abraham', visualizes the encounter of Abraham with his visitors under the tree at Mamre. It succeeds in expressing the invitation of the Trinity beautifully and visually. The three visitors to Abraham, who seem one moment to be men and the next angels, and the next the three persons of the Godhead, sit around the table on which food is placed. They seem to invite you in to occupy a fourth place, to share their food, their intimacy, their love, their life. In prayer you are being drawn into the divine loving, even when you cannot sense it. In the Eucharist you are being drawn into the divine loving, even when you forget it. Entering the mystery is exactly what God wants us to do. We do not need to hold back or be afraid. For we do not need to be worthy to enter. We need to be a little bit vulnerable, and who isn't? He draws us in with cords of love.

The fifth, final, thing is this. The love that draws us in, and never entirely lets us go, nevertheless sends us out, renewed and refreshed by our experience of the beauty, the holiness, the intimacy and the grace, filled with the love, to go with the flow of the love that runs over the earth. Each of us needs always to know that we are deeply loved, even when we mess up and therefore need the love the more, and to know ourselves to be channels of love. To every one of us, God who is Trinity says, 'Know yourself always deeply loved'; and whenever we are strong enough to hear it God adds: 'Go with the flow of that love, helping it to reach those margins of the world where people can hardly believe it is love for them.'

But the Christian tradition and indeed the Scriptures do not portray heaven as a place where God exists, living a Trinitarian life but otherwise alone. Instead there is a wonderful picture of God surrounded by the angels and the saints. Sometimes there is an emphasis on prayer and worship, sometimes on feasting. But always it is a picture of a social place, a community life. The Church imagines and senses a great company to which we are joined in one fellowship, especially when we pray and praise.

Very often we know very little about the saints and their lives on earth; many lived in this world a long time ago and their stories are lost in the mists of time. But we do know that they share the life of heaven and they belong with us in the communion of the saints. Just that. That is not very much, but it is more than enough. Of course, it is marvellous to have saints about whom are told heroic stories and edifying tales. But there is a danger that we begin to imagine that saints are those who catch our imagination, who attract us by their personality, who make us think 'if only I could follow their example'. But saints are not only, and not chiefly, like that.

In the end their example is not what matters. If truth be told, even when we know a good deal about their human exploits, the example is not always altogether useful, for most of these heroes of the past lived out their Christian pilgrimage in a world very different from ours. Even when we may genuinely benefit from the example of the saints, that is not what really matters. The greatest danger in laying emphasis on the lives they led, the things they did, and the example they left us, is that we trap the saints in the past. We think of them as Christians who lived 'once upon a time' but are no more. We trap them somewhere in remote Christian history.

But the wonderful thing about the saints is that they *are*, rather than they *were*. And the word that is the key to how they relate to us and why they matter is not example, but communion. The Apostles' Creed proclaims, 'I believe in the communion of saints'. It is our communion with the saints that is crucial – our fellowship with them. You cannot be in communion with those who are no more, only with the living, and the saints – the Christian dead, the 'faithful departed' as the Church often calls them – are, I believe, alive and well and saying their prayers.

When the Anglican Church came into its distinctive form at the Reformation in the sixteenth century, this important truth was in danger of being lost. In the centuries since it has often again been obscured. It was almost bound to be so because in the rejection, for truth's sake, of medieval excess the cult of the saints was pruned drastically. So concerned was the Church to lose the sort of prayers to the saints that put them in the place of God that it almost seemed incapable of thinking of the departed and of Christian prayer in the same breath. Yet the oldest tradition of prayer and the saints sees their prayer for us, and ours for them, as part of a natural expression of affection and solidarity in the great communion of saints. It is not about them granting favours. It is not about us needing prayers and they being beyond that need. It is quite simply about loving relationships in the family of Christ. It has been a great impoverishment of our theology and spirituality when we have failed to put in our liturgy words that express the loveliness of the mutual prayer that draws together the communion of saints and transcends barriers of time and place.

Archbishop Thomas Cranmer, that great architect of Anglican worship in the sixteenth century, expressed the purest theology of our relationship with the Christian dead in the opening lines of the collect he wrote for All Saints' Day: 'O Almighty God, who hast knit together thine elect in one communion and fellowship, in the mystical body of thy Son'. If God knits us together, he does so through the joyful mutuality of our prayers for one another, and through our common prayer and praise offered together, in communion, through Jesus Christ to the Father.

I want us to recover that sense of the communion of saints, of the holy ones of God as our companions, who *are*, rather than *were*, not only because it should boost our morale and give us joy, but also because it is important for the Church as it tries to share with people its deep conviction in eternal life. We live in an age in which there is uncertainty about life beyond death. While there are those who are convinced that there is nothing beyond the grave, there are a great many more who believe in eternal life of some kind, and in some sort of communion between those on earth and those beyond; but such belief is found in eccentric and even harmful forms. A world of spiritualism can thrive, and even seem to be meeting deep needs, where the Church's proclamation of its Easter faith is hesitant, impoverished and less than convincing. A Church that is joyfully alive with its belief in the communion of saints, with its conviction that we are close to the dead when we pray for them and with them, both proclaims an important theological truth and also meets a deep pastoral need.

One of the purest and most poetic expressions of how the Christian faith has understood the life of heaven and our communion with those who have died comes, perhaps surprisingly, not from the Catholic tradition that always has much to say about the saints but from the writings of the seventeenth-century Puritan Richard Baxter. Within his hymn, 'He wants [lacks] not friends that hath thy love', he writes:

> Within the fellowship of saints
> is wisdom, safety, and delight;
> and when my heart declines and faints,
> it's raisèd by their heat and light.
>
> As for my friends, they are not lost.
> The several vessels of thy fleet
> though parted now, by tempests tossed,
> shall safely in the haven meet.
>
> We still are centred all in thee,
> though distant, members of one Head;
> within one family we be,
> and by one faith and spirit led.

Before thy throne we daily meet
as joint-petitioners to thee;
in spirit each the other greet,
and shall again each other see.
'He wants not friends that hath thy love',
New English Hymnal

For Baxter part of his joy in the saints is the encouragement they give. Great figures of Christian heroism or quiet, determined faithful men and women of prayer, they inspire us to walk as they walked and to love as they loved. When our faith grows dark and cold, it is revived by their light and heat.

For me, as for Baxter, the commemoration of the saints is not just about the outstanding heroes of the faith. It is about 'my friends' who have gone through death. Those giant, heroic figures, the great company of the dead and we ourselves still here on earth, are not three categories of Christian, but one family, one fellowship, one communion. We belong together. The way we are held together is prayer. Lovingly we pray for those who have gone before us and we may trust that, in the loving providence of God, they lovingly pray for us, 'joint-petitioners', all caught up in mutual affection and devotion that breaks out in the prayer and praise of Christian worship every day.

The communion of saints is primarily about this 'cloud of witnesses', who belong together and draw us into their fellowship. We probably ought to be more interested in being fellow pilgrims in their company than in particular individuals. Nevertheless it has been a wise instinct through Christian history to hold on to the stories of some whose lives on earth have been most inspiring, speaking of them as 'saints' in a rather particular way and commemorating them in the Christian calendar, joining our prayers with theirs. God's purpose for us is that we shall always continue to be the unique individual persons he created us to be. Although we are drawn by God's love into deep communion with him, we do not lose our identity. It is because of this that we can make sense of ongoing relationships with particular saints who have, perhaps, featured in the history of our locality or given their name to the church where we worship, or simply share our name.

Among the saints with whom we have this communion is, of course, Mary the mother of Jesus. Although we know that God is not male and that patriarchal language about God needs to be balanced with some other more feminine insights, it is natural that Christians should invest Mary with some of their deepest emotions in relation to the feminine. For Catholic Christianity, Mary has always had a special place and the sense of her prayers is strong. Within the Reformed tradition, as a reaction against teaching about Mary that seemed to go beyond what Scripture could support, there has been a sad neglect, which has been a real loss. Ecumenical convergence is enabling us to leave that behind.

I want to explore some of the less common ways of speaking of Mary. Leaving on one side Mary as mother, Mary as virgin, Mary as the obedient one, Mary as the suffering one and much more, instead I want to look at three other aspects of her role in the Christian story.

First, Mary as collaborator. Here I have to take you to the annunciation story as reported in Luke 1, a scene so loved of artists with fair Gabriel and beautiful Mary visually in dialogue, though the conversation at a deeper level is between the peasant girl and her God. God has a divine purpose. God must come among his people in the person of the Son to be their Saviour. And God has a plan. God will be born as a human baby; he will, as Paul says in Galatians 4, 'be born of a woman'. And how is that going to be? Through the collaboration of Mary of Nazareth, whom the angel tells us is 'full of grace' even before the Holy Spirit has come upon her and the power of the Most High has overshadowed her.

The language used in the annunciation story, although it is not exactly about invitation and acceptance (in the end God is saying what he wants), gives the sense of a God who is looking for one who will collaborate with him. Traditionally we speak of Mary's words – 'Behold the handmaid of the Lord; be it unto me according to thy word' (Luke 1.38, AV) – as her obedience. But to me her 'Yes' is something much more exciting and life-giving than a kind of resigned obedience. It is the 'Yes' of the willing collaborator, the co-worker. Perhaps a Mary full of grace was bound to say 'Yes', but in a way I want to cling to the idea of a God who holds his breath waiting and hoping that it will be 'Yes' that she says. And God is not disappointed. The Incarnation comes about through a wonderful partnership of the human and the divine, the Holy Spirit and the Virgin; the initiative is God's, of course, but the human response is vital to the enterprise. And because it was a wonderful partnership of the human and the divine, its fruit was Jesus Christ, truly God and truly a man, utterly and equally human and divine.

The second picture of Mary is as prophet. The world of the Bible is a man's domain and the voice of women is often silenced. There are a few heroines of the Old Covenant – Deborah, Hannah, Judith, Esther, in the Old Testament – but they are the exceptions. It is fascinating to study the extraordinary first chapter of Matthew's Gospel, with its list of men who 'begat', all the generations from Abraham to Jesus. There is much about the men, the ones who begat, and not much about the women who laboured to bring each new son to birth. But in this fascinating genealogy just occasionally a woman gets a mention – Tamar, who was involved in incest, Rahab, the prostitute who helped the Israelites to capture Jericho, Ruth, the outsider who came home with the widowed Naomi, Bathsheba, seduced by King David. It is an extraordinary list of marginalized women and none of them has a voice. But then there is Mary, another marginalized woman, the one found pregnant before she and Joseph had come together, the one to be set aside and divorced quietly. And suddenly Mary, in an ecstatic dialogue with her cousin Elizabeth, another marginalized woman, despised for her barrenness, finds her voice. She sings her song, making the protest and speaking the prophecy for the marginalized, poor and downtrodden. It is a woman's voice. The prophets of old were men – Isaiah and Jeremiah, Micah and Hosea, Ezekiel and Malachi and more – but now, in that authentic tradition of spokespeople of the Lord, comes Mary the prophet.

The danger is that we are so used to hearing this protest song from Luke 1, the Magnificat that the Church sings every evening and has made safe with musical melodies, that we do not hear its radical message and its challenge. This is the song of feminine humanity, of downtrodden humanity that has found its voice:

> He has looked with favour on the lowliness of his servant.
> Surely, from now on all generations will call me blessed;
> for the Mighty One has done great things for me . . .
> He has shown strength with his arm;
> he has scattered the proud in the thoughts of their hearts.
> He has brought down the powerful from their thrones,
> and lifted up the lowly;

he has filled the hungry with good things,
and sent the rich away empty.

(Luke 1.48–49, 51–53)

Here stands this pregnant woman, carrying a child but not preoccupied with herself, utterly engaged with God's justice, God's
bias for the poor, God's judgement on the exploiters. She is the
articulate herald of a new order, the one that her Son will bring
into being.

The third image is of Mary as God-bearer. In Greek the word is
theotokos, the one who carries God. It is the ultimate description of
Mary. Because she is full of grace, because of her role as collaborator,
the Spirit works in her and she carried in her womb the one who is
as much God as he is human, Jesus Christ. There's a lovely description of this in Elizabeth Jennings' poem, 'The annunciation':

> It is a human child she loves,
> though a God stirs beneath her breast
> and great salvations grip her side.
> Elizabeth Jennings, in *A Sense of the World*

I want to say just two things about this profound title of God-bearer.
First, simply that it is worth holding on to, using with thankful
devotion when you think of Mary or see her portrayed in art. At
the very heart of faith, she is not what matters. She is simply a
vessel, a vessel for the divine and the means by which God came
uniquely among a people in a way that has changed everything.
Because she was that vessel, all generations are to call her blessed.
But she does not point to herself. She carries Christ into the world.
That was how he was first among his people, hidden in the Virgin's
womb.

The second thing is that it is like that again now. Christ's glory
fills the universe, but he is not seen on earth as he was in the
days of his Incarnation. Yes, his glory fills the universe, but he is
among his people, hidden, not in their wombs but in their hearts
and minds and bodies, and wherever they go they carry Christ
into the dark and hurting places, the unexpecting places of the world.
In other words, for all the uniqueness of Mary as *theotokos*, we also
are to be 'God-bearers', to carry Christ into every place and every
circumstance where people long for the love, compassion and life of
the Trinity.

For me Mary is a sister in the communion of saints. As she walks with us on our pilgrimage, just by her presence in our company she gently reminds us that we are also called to be collaborators, prophets and 'God-bearers'. Such thoughts of her raise our hearts to heaven but they also challenge us, like her, to establish the kingdom of heaven on earth. That too involves collaboration with God: a prophetic witness and a willingness to carry Christ into unexpecting places. And she is but one, though a particularly special one, of a great company of those who, long before they came to enjoy the life of heaven, played their part in growing the kingdom of heaven on earth.

But, as the previous chapter argued, the kingdom of God on earth is a beautiful but fragile phenomenon, not a universal 'age of gold'. The kingdom of heaven is indeed on earth, and has been in every generation, but it is to be found in pockets and in breakings-in and our task is simply to defend those pockets and to work with God, with patience and passion to create new spaces where it may break in.

The Gospels speak of the kingdom of God being 'at hand'. Both John the Baptist and Jesus speak in these terms. The way the Scriptures portray it, there are moments when the kingdom seems to have been brought in by the presence of Jesus, other moments when it appears to be just around the corner and some occasions when it seems that it must wait for a mighty intervention at the end of time. And there is something of an ambivalence about this kingdom, just as there is about the kingship of the one whose kingdom it is. Jesus, the one who inaugurates the kingdom, is himself one who is variously pictured as in our midst, near and coming on the clouds of heaven at the end of time.

There is a strong insistence that the kingdom is among us. 'Great in your midst is the Holy One of Israel,' says Isaiah 12.6. There is a sense that the new age of heaven on earth has begun. Jesus himself tells us, in Matthew 28, that he will be with us 'till the end of time' and it is part of the Christian paradox that the one who says that he will return also says that he will never be away. Our future hope for the kingdom arises from our present experience of the reality of God, who at one level does not have to come because he is so firmly among us always, with signs everywhere, however small and hidden, of his kingdom.

But there is always a sense of something just around the corner. 'Rejoice in the Lord always; again I will say, Rejoice,' says Paul writing to the Philippians. 'Let your gentleness be known to everyone. The Lord is near' (Philippians 4.4–5). Although it is true that the kingdom is around us, there is a sense in which it renews its impact in a flash and reasserts itself in a fresh way. We encounter it in the person about to turn the corner towards us, in the events a few days hence, in the conversation we shall be drawn into, in the moment of stillness we shall try to create, in the glimpse of joy like a shaft of light, in the moment of peace in the bearing of long and wearying pain. In all of these, metaphorically 'just around the corner', we may meet the Lord coming towards us, drawing us into the kingdom.

There is also a powerful and dramatic scene of a kingdom that seems much further away in terms of time. The prophets love to picture this new age, when God's salvation will be experienced, and they do so in passages where the future tense is pregnant with promise. Thus, for instance, Zephaniah can speak of that day when the Lord

> will rejoice over you with gladness,
> he will renew you in his love;
> he will exult over you with loud singing
> as on a day of festival.
> I will remove disaster from you,
> so that you will not bear reproach for it.
> I will deal with all your oppressors
> at that time.
> And I will save the lame
> and gather the outcast,
> and I will change their shame into praise
> and renown in all the earth.
> At that time I will bring you home,
> at the time when I gather you.
> (Zephaniah 3.17–20)

This is the God of the future tense, who will rejoice, will renew, will exult, will remove, will deal, will save, will gather, will change and will bring home. However much we rejoice to see the in-breaking of the kingdom in life around us, there is always a sense of expectancy and longing for something that is yet to come. 'Glory to the Father, and to the Son and to the Holy Spirit, as it was in the beginning, is now and shall be for ever' can have a somewhat static feel to it. But the 'shall be for ever' is the future of the God who will do new things. That is the picture, from Revelation 21, with which this chapter began, the creation of a new heaven and new earth.

> Then I saw a new heaven and a new earth; for the first heaven and the first earth had passed away, and the sea was no more. And I saw the holy city, the new Jerusalem, coming down out of heaven from God, prepared as a bride adorned for her husband.   (Revelation 21.1–2)

Whatever exactly the vision meant to John, and however we interpret it and passages like it that speak puzzlingly of the end of the world order as we know it, the overwhelming sense is of a God who still has surprises for his creation. When it comes to divine activity, and especially to establishing the kingdom of heaven on earth, you can almost hear God say, 'You haven't seen the half of it yet.'

So our task – and it is, in reality, more joy than task – is to go on holding before us the vision of the kingdom of heaven and the communion of the saints, and to seek to advance that kingdom and communion on earth. We do it by entering the life of the Trinity from which love flows to the earth, by speaking of God with clarity and conviction, by trying to discern God's will for the earth, by resisting evil in ourselves and in our society and by striving for peace and justice.

But above all we do it by letting God be God, with all his yearning, his loving and his transforming beauty. We need to make space for God to be, to act and to draw the world to himself, establishing in human hearts on earth the glory of heaven and, in so doing, setting forward God's kingdom – on earth as it is in heaven.

References

Common Worship. London, Church House Publishing, 2000.

Common Worship: Christian Initiation. London, Church House Publishing, 2005.

Common Worship: Ordination Services. London, Church House Publishing, 2007.

Hopkins, Gerard Manley, 'God's Grandeur', *The Faber Book of Religious Verse*. London, Faber, 1972.

Jennings, Elizabeth, *A Sense of the World*. London, Carcanet, 1958.

New English Hymnal. Norwich, Canterbury Press, 1986.

Teilhard de Chardin, Pierre, 'Mass on the world', in *Hymn of the Universe*. London, Collins, 1965.

Vanstone, W. H., *Love's Endeavour, Love's Expense*. London, Darton, Longman and Todd, 1977.

Weston, Frank, 'Our present duty', speech at the Anglo-Catholic Congress, 1923 <http://anglicanhistory.org/weston/weston2.html>.

Acknowledgements

The publisher and author acknowledge with thanks permission to reproduce copyright material. Every effort has been made to acknowledge fully the sources of material reproduced in this book. The publisher apologizes for any omissions that may remain and, if notified, will ensure that full acknowledgements are made in a subsequent edition.

Unless otherwise noted, Scripture quotations are taken from the New Revised Standard Version of the Bible, Anglicized Edition, copyright © 1989, 1995 by the Division of Christian Education of the National Council of the Churches of Christ in the USA. Used by permission. All rights reserved.

Two extracts (marked AV) are from the Authorized Version of the Bible (The King James Bible), the rights in which are vested in the Crown, and are reproduced by permission of the Crown's Patentee, Cambridge University Press.

Extracts from *Common Worship* are copyright © The Archbishops' Council, 2000, and are reproduced by permission.

Extracts from *Common Worship: Christian Initiation* are copyright © The Archbishops' Council, 2005, and are reproduced by permission.

Extracts from *Common Worship: Ordination Services* are copyright © The Archbishops' Council, 2007, and are reproduced by permission.

'Love's endeavour, love's expense' is taken from *Love's Endeavour, Love's Expense*, by W. H. Vanstone, published and copyright © 1977 by Darton, Longman and Todd Ltd, London, and is used by permission of the publishers.

'The annunciation' is taken from *New Collected Poems*, by Elizabeth Jennings, published 2002 by Carcanet, London, and is reproduced by permission of David Higham Associates Ltd.

Also available

Glory in Our Midst treats the period from the beginning of Advent to the very end of Christmas and Epiphany as a single unit. The author explores how, gradually, the meaning of Christ's coming is revealed and, behind that unfolding, how key elements emerge in the Christian understanding of God himself.

Michael Perham, Bishop of Gloucester, is well known for his many reflective and liturgical publications, which have inspired, challenged, strengthened and nourished many on their spiritual journeys.

He writes:

> For me the weeks from Advent to Candlemas are full of delight. The biblical stories they recall are full of fascination, the liturgy of the seasons is rich and many-layered and the theological truths about the one whose glory is in our midst are exciting to share. Good news always needs to be proclaimed.

Glory in our Midst is accessible and readable; it can be read from cover to cover or used meditatively throughout the Advent season, taking us daily more deeply into the mystery of the Incarnation, and inspiring us to make it a real and vivid part of our lives.